THE
ELUSIVE
MR. WESLEY

JOHN WESLEY HIS OWN BIOGRAPHER

VOLUME ONE

THE ELUSIVE MR. WESLEY

JOHN WESLEY HIS OWN BIOGRAPHER

Richard P. Heitzenrater

Abingdon Press
Nashville

THE ELUSIVE MR. WESLEY

VOLUME I

Copyright © 1984 by Abingdon Press

Library of Congress Cataloging in Publication Data

HEITZENRATER, RICHARD P., 1939–
  John Wesley his own biographer.
  (The Elusive Mr. Wesley; v. 1)
  Includes selections from the writings of John Wesley.
  Bibliography: p.
  1. Wesley, John, 1703–1791. 2. Methodist Church—England—
  Clergy—Biography. I. Title. II. Wesley, John, 1703–1791. Selections.
  1984. III. Series: Heitzenrater, Richard P., 1939–   Elusive Mr.
  Wesley; v. 1.
  BX8495.W5H43 vol. 1   287'.092'4s [B]   83-25882
                          [287'.092'4] [B]

ISBN 0-687-11554-X (pbk.)

MANUFACTURED BY THE PARTHENON PRESS AT
NASHVILLE, TENNESSEE, UNITED STATES OF AMERICA

To my family
for their encouragement
and support of my continuing pursuit
of the elusive Mr. Wesley

CONTENTS

LIST OF ILLUSTRATIONS

PREFACE

Every generation discovers the past for itself. The process can be as simple as repeating long-held traditions or as complicated as tracing centuries-old genealogies. The historian's task is to help disentangle fact from fantasy in our various rehearsals of past events. In a sense, this book is intended to encourage the reader to participate in the historian's craft, by exhibiting some of the problems confronted, the methods used, the conclusions reached, and the loose ends left dangling when one tries to uncover the past "as it really happened."

The focus of our study is John Wesley, the "founder" of Methodism. Our quest is a part of the current interest in discovering "roots"—in this case, the roots of a particular religious heritage. My introduction to this adventure came some fifteen years ago when I accepted the challenge of decoding Wesley's previously unpublished personal diaries. Struggling through the ciphers, shorthands, and symbols of these fascinating private documents, I became increasingly aware that the emerging image of the young man Wesley was quite different in many ways from the typical portrayals in most biographies of the man. To add to the confusion, Wesley's own later recollections at times differed in significant ways from some of these early daily records of his activities.

As my efforts to reconstruct an accurate portrait of the

young Wesley broadened into a study of the whole of his life and thought, I discovered further problems. The confusion evident among contemporary observers of Wesley was only compounded by the variety of sometimes conflicting images given to the public over the subsequent two centuries by artists, biographers, historians, and iconographers. Over three hundred studies of Wesley have been written, many of them more confusing than helpful in the process of trying to recapture a historically accurate basis upon which to build a fully adequate picture of the man. The consternation caused by such a lack of consensus has given rise to my fascination with what might be called "the search for the real John Wesley."

The biographer's endeavor is similar in many ways to the task of the portrait painter; both try to help us see beyond the obvious to the essential. But every such interpretive attempt, to be adequately edifying, should be based on full and accurate information. During the last two decades, an increasing number of critical studies of Wesley have provided helpful information in this regard, though not always noticed by the biographers. Future studies will also benefit from the completion of the new critical edition of Wesley's works now in progress. In the meantime, however, we can try to work our way toward a better understanding of Wesley by recognizing that our currently popular portraits of Wesley are shaped in large part by nineteenth- and early twentieth-century stereotypes that were constructed with a specific apologetic purpose in mind. We need also to keep in mind that some parts of the well-rehearsed Wesley story are based on little or no hard evidence and have become part of the time-honored tradition simply through repetition—the succession of twice-told tales soon taking on the appearance of historical fact.

This work attempts to help the reader discover Wesley anew by displaying a unique combination of material, some of it quite familiar, some readily accessible but generally unfamiliar and waiting rediscovery, and some only recently discovered and never before published. Volume I contains selections from Wesley's own writings, providing the basis for his developing portrait, while at the same time showing how some aspects of the Wesley "legend" began to develop. Volume II focuses on accounts written by his contemporaries; these fill in additional details, occasionally providing a helpful corrective to Wesley's own self-portrait as well as illustrating the wide variety of reactions to Wesley by friend and foe. Volume II also traces the history of Wesley studies, showing how he has fared in the eyes of historians and biographers through successive generations of interpretation.

Having thus surveyed many of the ways in which Wesley saw himself, looked at the variety of descriptions of him by his contemporaries, and examined the manner in which he has been treated by a host of writers down through the years, the reader will have begun to grasp the major events and issues of Wesley's life and thought, as well as to discover that the possibility of recapturing the "real" John Wesley is an elusive ideal that has never been (and perhaps never can be) totally comprehended by any single book, at any given time, in any one place. Though many good books on Wesley have been written, this study will, I hope, demonstrate why it is difficult to suggest any one book that will satisfactorily "explain" the whole Wesley, and will also act as a critical guide through the maze of published material available on Wesley. At the same time, I hope that this effort will also introduce many people to the excitement of discovering John Wesley for themselves.

I wish to thank the many people who have aided and encouraged me in this work, especially Professor Albert C. Outler, whose expertise provided many suggestions that helped shape and refine the manuscript; Professor Frank Baker, whose mastery of detail has continued to help me discover John Wesley; Professor John Walsh, whose insight and advice helped me shape the project; my assistant Wanda Willard Smith, whose proficiency in the topic made the deadlines manageable; and my wife, Karen, whose editorial skills preserved me from many infelicities of style.

R.P.H.

Southern Methodist University
May 1, 1983

The Rev.ᵈ JOHN WESLEY, M.A.

Bodlidge sculp, King Street, Upper Moor Fields

Wesley published this portrait of himself during the first year of his monthly *Arminian Magazine* (1778) as an initial response to a reader's request for "pictures or other decorations or embellishments." In spite of receiving Wesley's own stamp of approval at the time, the likeness apparently was ill-received by the readers (see below, page 25).

INTRODUCTION:
THE ELUSIVE MR. WESLEY

"His history, if well written," concludes the writer of Wesley's lengthy obituary in the *Gentleman's Magazine,* "will certainly be important, for in every respect, as the founder of the most numerous sect in the kingdom, as a man, and as a writer, he must be considered as one of the most extraordinary characters this or any age ever produced." This piece of effusive eloquence is perhaps only slightly exaggerated. John Wesley has come to be known as one of the major figures of the eighteenth century, his impact being felt both in Great Britain and in America. He played a major role as one of the leaders of the evangelical revival that swept much of the Protestant world in his day. His literary production was prolific, and writings such as his *Journal* are still seen as models of eighteenth-century style.

But Wesley's importance goes beyond the realm of literature and religion. Concerned with such issues as education, prison conditions, and poverty, he played an important role in the development of early social reforms in an increasingly industrialized society. Trained at Christ Church, Oxford, he was intrigued by the current trends of science and medicine, and he published many popular treatises on diverse subjects ranging from experiments in electricity to home remedies for the gout. He produced a flood of pamphlets on a wide assortment of topics ranging from linguistics to music. As a recognized leader among the people, he entered into the political swirl surrounding the revolutionary movements of his day, offering his services to the king to raise a regiment of troops to fight the French, and giving his advice to the colonial secretary on the explosive matter of the American revolt.

Wesley sensed the spirit of the English people perhaps as well as any person in his day. The true nature of his own mind and spirit, however, appears somewhat more elusive. His own breast felt the heartbeat of a staunchly loyal Tory; yet he could feel well the pulse of a nation that stirred with the rumblings of revolution. He was able to remain an Anglican clergyman to his dying breath and at the same time harness the energies of revival into a new form that was to become a major force in Protestant Christianity as Methodism.

From the very beginning of his public activities, Wesley was a controversial figure. Persons of differing religious and political persuasions did not hesitate to attack him in print as well as in person. His fledgling movement was already being decried in the newspapers in 1732, and his character was publicly slandered and attacked in court as early as 1737. Through all the controversies he was not without supporters; every spirited attack elicited a zealous defense that tended to bolster the developing Wesley legend. At his death, friend and foe alike rushed to produce biographical portraits of the Wesley *they* knew. From the beginning, the descriptions of Wesley presented to the public have caused no small amount of confusion, as well as controversy, as successive generations have tried to sift through the various accounts of this complex and rather elusive man, looking for the "real" John Wesley.

The Quest of the "Real" John Wesley

The problems confronting persons looking for the "real" John Wesley are typified in the attempt to find an "accurate" pictorial representation of the man. Dismissing for the moment the problems faced by nineteenth- and twentieth-century artists who tried to depict Wesley long after his death, we would expect to find some standard, recognizable visage among the eighteenth-century portraits of Wesley. The wide variety of images that confront us, even among portraits done by the best artists of the day (many of whom were looking directly at the man as they painted), is confusing and serves to symbolize and illustrate the larger problem of trying to catch the essence of his life and thought. There is no consensus in either case, visual or interpretive, and the variety of representations can be disconcerting.

In the search for the elusive John Wesley, the question of physical appearance is more than just the passing fancy of an antiquarian historian. It is, among other things, one indication of the limits of factual information that might be retrieved from a given period. For example, we might ask the simple question, What color was Wesley's hair when he was a young man? One eyewitness, who lived under the same roof with him in Georgia in 1737, referred to his "Adonis locks of *auburn* hair . . . which he took infinite pains to have in the most exact order." Just a few years later (1744) another eyewitness, describing Wesley's appearance in the pulpit of St. Mary's, Oxford, mentioned in particular his "*black* hair quite smooth, parted very exactly." The contradiction of these two literary descriptions is further confused by a third impression, portrayed on canvas by John Williams at about the same time (1741). The painting does exhibit the neatness of Wesley's hair, as mentioned by the other observers, but shows the color to be black in general, with a brownish tint where the light reflects off the curls and waves. On the basis of the contemporary sources of evidence, we are left with no definitive answer to the question.

The problem of hair color is difficult in one sense because few descriptions (literary or graphic) were drawn up of Wesley as a young man. The portraits proliferate as he grew older and more famous. The problem of hair color disappears, since his hair turned gray and then white. But another, even more surprising problem arises. Among the dozens of paintings, drawings, busts, and other representations, there is little or no consensus as to Wesley's facial features. The most one can say is that he apparently had a rather prominent, pointed nose. This, combined with the usual portrayal of his hair as long with curls on the end, and the almost universal presence of Geneva bands around his neck, gives a note of uniformity and recognition to a vast array of portraits that otherwise do not much resemble one another. In some cases, on these grounds alone, portraits have occasionally been identified as "possibly" representing John Wesley, even though the general impression would otherwise cause the viewer to be skeptical. The problem was somewhat upsetting to some nineteenth-century British Methodists who, in the face of such confusing evidence, commissioned an artist to create a "standard" portrait of Wesley in the 1820s, a generation after his death. The resulting "synthetic" portrait (see volume 2, page 181) was conceded by most to be notably unconvincing as a replica of Wesley's visage and was unable to garner lasting support as a standard portrait.

Our inability to specify with any assurance the color of Wesley's hair or the exact nature of his visage is, perhaps, a minor point. Nevertheless, it does suggest the sense of caution with which we should approach our attempt to discover the "facts" on other, perhaps more significant questions, even when we are using firsthand, eyewitness accounts (*about,* or even *by,* Wesley). A simple illustration can be seen in the question of Wesley's name (see below, page 37). Contemporary evidence, usually very illuminating and valuable, can also at times be skimpy, inaccurate, misleading, contradictory, and confusing. Although often the best source of information, primary source material must be used critically and carefully.

In trying to sort through the contemporary accounts of Wesley's activities, character, and significance, one must do more than merely differentiate those views that attack him from those that defend him. In some cases, the most virulent attack or vicious satire may, in fact, be built upon some grain of truth that might be overlooked in a more favorable description of the man. Most biographers have either disregarded Wesley's detractors as a source of information, or seen their attacks as simply spurious fabrications, and have been willing to rely almost entirely on the defenders of Wesley for their view of the situation. But what judge would ever assume that the defense, no matter how pious, was by nature or necessity the only reliable source of believable or factual information?

To make the matter more complicated, both Wesley's enemies and friends were attracted to him not only by who or what he *actually* was (if that could in fact ever be known for sure), but by what they (and he) *thought* he was. Observations of contemporaries can, of course, be analyzed on the basis of their known prejudices and purposes. But these same guidelines must also be applied to Wesley's own descriptions of himself; his autobiographical comments need always to be tested against other available evidence.

In some cases, Wesley makes statements that either can be easily misinterpreted or simply exhibit a bad memory. For instance, he mentions in his *Journal* that in 1771 he visited South Leigh, adding that "here it was that I preached my first sermon, six and forty years ago." Based on this reference, biographers have assumed that Wesley must have preached there the first Sunday after his ordination in 1725. A brass plaque on the pulpit of that church still proclaims this to be the case. However, Wesley's own handwritten copy of his first sermon (with his note on the cover, "The first sermon I ever wrote") tells another story. It lists on the back the places and occasions of preaching, with South Leigh listed as the *ninth* occasion, in *1727*. This does in a sense confirm that Wesley "preached his first sermon" in South Leigh, but it was not his first occasion for preaching, nor his first preaching of that first sermon!

Biographers have often repeated many such inaccuracies and half-truths and have magnified many of the legends that sprang up in Wesley's own day; then they have often recast all these to fit their own purposes. Many an account of Wesley is but an editorial gloss on the man, an attempt on the part of an author to prove some point about either Wesley's thought or, more likely and less obviously, the author's own. By careful selection and editing, an author can make Wesley appear in a number of guises. Our task is to recognize as many of the guises as possible, then to ferret out the *dis*guises in which he has been placed, and thereby to discover as accurately as possible the full range of thought and activity that characterize this remarkable man.

One of our primary tasks, then, in trying to discover the elusive John Wesley is to recognize that *all* the information that comes to us must be examined critically, no matter whether it was written by Wesley himself, recounted by an eyewitness (friendly or otherwise), or compiled years after the events. No single type of source, in and of itself, is necessarily a sufficient resource for our quest. Firsthand accounts are in many ways, of course, the best, but are not without problems of bias and shortsightedness in that they are in some cases too close to the events they describe. Secondary accounts, while suffering from the problems of historical distance, might at the same time benefit from the more inclusive objectivity that such hindsight makes possible. Taken as a whole, these materials provide a vast amount of information that must be sifted carefully by the observer with an eye toward discovering a full and accurate basis upon which to develop a credible and edifying picture of the man and his times.

Having recognized the problems of personal bias in the sources we are using, we must also then realize that the same problem will exist in the mind of the person examining the materials. We all come at historical data with certain prejudices, sometimes anticipating the results of our investigation, while at other times actually molding the material to fit our own preconceptions. Recognizing these tendencies, and consciously resisting the temptation to impose our own biases onto the historical material, we must realize the result of our quest might not be what we expect or even desire. Especially when looking at primary documents for the first time, we must expect surprises. Such expectations of the unexpected make the historical enterprise both exciting and rewarding.

Considerations in the Quest for Historical Accuracy

The success of any exploratory journey depends not only on the selection of a potentially fruitful direction of enquiry but also on careful preparation. Wesley's recognized significance as a historical figure and the wide variety of sources available for our study almost guarantee the value of our venture for the person interested in discovering John Wesley. But the confusing variety of images of Wesley portrayed in his own day as well as over the past two centuries gives us some pause as we start on this journey. Part of our preparation must include the anticipation of problems that will confront us in our quest of the elusive John Wesley.

There are several reasons why Wesley was and is a rather elusive figure, as a person, as a leader, as a writer. Some of these are normal considerations that confront almost any attempt to reconstruct the life and thought of a historic person. Other situations are more particular to Wesley's own situation. In every case, a recognition of these considerations will make the search for an accurate and full basis for the portrayal of Wesley, though perhaps no easier, more fruitful.

1) *Wesley was a legend in his own day.* He had a heroic public image based on a life-style that approached epic proportions. The traditional rehearsal of the statistics of his life speaks for itself: 250,000 miles traveled on horseback, over 40,000 sermons preached during a span of sixty-six years, more than 400 publications on nearly every conceivable topic, all of this activity continuing almost to his dying day in his eighty-eighth year. These are the marks of a man certain to appear larger than life-size, in spite of his small physical stature (five feet three inches, 126 pounds). Never mind that some of those miles in later life were actually covered in a finely appointed chaise or that many of those publications were extracts from other authors or quite brief tracts. These statistics still represent a monumental production for one lifetime, and many of the people of his day, though perhaps not familiar with the precise statistics, were aware of Wesley's

reputation as a notoriously busy, seemingly tireless person who was always on the move.

To say that Wesley's reputation may have outstripped his "real" capabilities (an element of any legendary status) is not to say that we must disregard or throw aside any resource that tends toward hyperbole. What people (as well as Wesley) believed to be true about him is an important consideration in his own autobiographical development, in the flow of historical events around him, and in our attempt to understand the whole story. One of the most ticklish tasks that confronts the historian in reconstructing the past is to sort through various perceptions of reality as expressed by contemporary participants and observers, for each of whom, we should remember, reality was based upon whatever they believed to be true.

Wesley himself seems to have adopted a self-perception that was based upon, or at least contributed to, a heroic image. His writings often contain autobiographical recollections that reflect a somewhat magnified, or perhaps idealized, view of his character or personality. This tendency resulted in part from the necessity of defending himself in the forum of public opinion. Part of his apologetic method was quite naturally to put forth his best side whenever possible, even if his editorial management of the truth might result in some distortion of the historical facts.

In spite of his good intentions, Wesley's accounts of himself are occasionally marked by discrepancies and contradictions that at times tend to inflate his good image. A simple example of this can be seen in Wesley's sermon "Redeeming the Time," in which he promotes the virtues of rising early in the morning. He cites his own experience at Oxford as an example of one practical way to discover just how much (or little) sleep a person needs each night. His solution to the problem of spending more time in bed than was necessary (indicated in part by persistent insomnia) was to procure an alarm that woke him an hour earlier each morning for four or five days until he settled on an hour of rising that suited both his physical and spiritual needs—4:00 A.M. A good story to illustrate a good point. As for the historical facts of the matter, Wesley in his diary had recorded the process of working back toward the 4:00 A.M. rising time as a gradual development that took place over several months. In the sermon illustration, he simply telescoped several months into four days, making a much better story, but at the same time giving a picture of himself that is perhaps more remarkable than the facts warrant. The main point being made in the sermon is no less true, but the illustrative story should not be taken either as a historical episode in its details or as an accurate indication of Wesley's capacity for effecting instant solutions. That the people (and perhaps even Wesley himself) came to believe these stories to be accurate representations of his character is, however, a fact that must be considered in our attempt to recover the perceptions of the eighteenth century.

Wesley's heroic image was built in part upon his own inclination toward seeing himself as a martyr. This self-impression is not often explicit in his own writings. He did, however, often express the opinion that persecution was a necessary mark of a true Christian, and his *Journal* is in one sense a lengthy rehearsal of events that display in great detail the confirmation of that truth in his own life.

The underlying tone of these accounts is perhaps as revealing as the actual content. For example, his narrative of the riots at Wednesbury (see page 125 below) concludes with a comment that indicates Wesley was not at all ruffled by the violent physical struggles that had just occurred. He then goes on to analyze the various ways in which God's providence might be perceived as evident in those events. His brother's journal for that period records an even more telling reflection; there Charles indicates that his brother John understood how the early Christian martyrs could stand in the persecutors' flames and not feel any pain. Wesley's self-perceptions of this sort could not help finding their way into the consciousness of the public, and the biblical allusions and martyr-like experiences were certainly not lost on them.

2) *Wesley's public image can be distinguished from his private image.* This rather commonplace observation could be

made about almost any famous person and is mentioned here simply because it is often overlooked in many studies of Wesley. His own writings display this point rather nicely. The "public" documents, such as his sermons and journal, at times give quite a different picture from that contained in his "private" documents, such as his letters and diaries. To say this is not to imply any devious intent on Wesley's part. Rather, the distinction between the two images is based upon the difference in design and intent of these two types of material. Sermons designed for the propagation of practical divinity, whether preached or published, have quite different perimeters of self-revelation from letters written to one's brother in the depths of despair. To read each with an eye toward discerning the "actual" situation being described, we must have an analytical sensitivity to the circumstances out of which the writing was generated. Such is also the case when we look at the writings of contemporary observers who claim to be able to describe the private, as distinguished from the public, image of a person.

Wesley's public image, nearly legendary in scope and proportion, certainly fed the tendency toward hero worship on the part of many of his followers. But at the same time, the exaggerated picture of piety and perfection inherent in such a perception of the man served to fuel the antagonism expressed by many of his detractors. Many critics inflamed the imagination of the public by contrasting this public, almost unreal image, with a demonic portrait of the "real" nature and intentions of the private person that lurked behind that public image. These attacks, often dismissed by Wesleyan adherents as the work of twisted minds, we should not simply discard out of hand without first recognizing that the sale and popularity of such writings, scurrilous as they may seem, depended upon their having a degree of credibility in the public eye. Just as there was a public image of Wesley that approached sainthood and was undergirded by a repertoire of appropriate anecdotes, there was also a public view of him that resembled a dangerous, ranting enthusiast and could believe the vilest of epithets. Both were flawed interpretations, yet both gained that degree of credibility because they

Wesley published this portrait of himself (artist unknown) in 1779 to replace the earlier portrait in *The Arminian Magazine* (see above, page 14). About the engravings in the *Magazine,* he told the readers in 1781, "I'll have better or none at all" (but see below, page 197).

contained a kernel of truth. The task of the careful historian is to try to discern just what the kernel of truth might be in specific instances that would allow seemingly obvious scurrility (or exaggerated virtue) to pass for a believable representation.

One might note in passing that many of the persons who were quite ready to attack Wesley in the public eye and do almost anything in their power to bring ridicule upon him and his movement found it difficult if not impossible to attack him privately as a person. This may, in part, reflect Wesley's own method of disputation, focusing on principles rather than personalities, but also may demonstrate a recognition of Wesley's personal integrity even by most of his enemies. This tendency to distinguish between the private and the public Mr. Wesley, for better or worse, is only one part of the larger picture of his controversial involvements, which have even wider repercussions in the attempt to discover the elusive John Wesley.

3) *Wesley was a controversial figure.* This consideration, like the last two points, is by no means a new observation on the life of John Wesley. But likewise, it carries with it certain implications that are often overlooked by persons trying to recapture an accurate picture of the man.

Wesley faced opposition from many quarters on a variety of issues. From the very beginning, the attacks came from both inside and outside the movement. The Oxford Methodists were not "of one mind," in spite of Wesley's oft-repeated comment to that effect; his own diary shows members who were "piqued" at his bolting from his group and even in one case writing a theme "against the Methodists." As the movement grew and developed, some of Wesley's preachers challenged his ideas and leadership, especially in the 1750s and 1760s. His brother Charles often disagreed with him on important matters of policy and procedure. The continuing reaction to many of Wesley's controversial actions and ideas during his lifetime set the stage for many of the disputes within the movement after his death.

The external attacks came from several directions, including opposite ends of the theological, political, and social spectra. Wesley was portrayed by different opponents in a mind-boggling variety of garbs; he was seen as a Quaker by some, a Papist by others, a ranting enthusiast by many, and an upper-crust snob by others. To discover the real Wesley simply on the basis of these attacks is of course impossible, even though they might unwittingly tell us something useful about the public's perception of him, as we have seen.

The writings generated by these controversies, however, should not be overlooked as a valuable source of information in our quest. Although they present a confusing picture in many ways, a careful look at this material will tell us quite a bit about the inner character of Wesley's life and thought, and particularly about his intellectual methodology. The writings include not only the attacks by Wesley's opponents and the defense by Wesley, but also the observations of many third parties, some quite obviously friendly to Wesley's cause but others less certain about their affiliation. The problem facing us is not to decide who is friend or foe, or to figure out who is right or wrong. Rather, we must decide what the attacks and the friendly defenses can tell us about Wesley, and what we can discern about Wesley from his writings in his own defense.

Wesley's own writings have caused the most problems for some recent authors who have been quick to point out that his controversial works (which represent a significant proportion) do not seem to maintain or develop any sort of consistent or systematic treatment of the major themes in Christian doctrine. It is difficult at best for a person to find anything approaching a well-developed system of thought, easily defined as "Wesleyan," in the whole of his works. Therefore many conclude that Wesley was not a major thinker of any significance. In the writings that arise from his many controversies, Wesley does appear from time to time to have made statements that even seem to be quite contradictory, in tone or emphasis at least, if not in substance. Some scholars, therefore, treat Wesley as a self-contradicting, confusing intellectual "lightweight," and dismiss him with comments such as that of Ronald Knox, who said that Wesley "is not a good advertisement for reading on horse-back."

We should not be too quick, however, to pass judgment on Wesley based only on someone's evaluation of the "rightness" or "wrongness" of his positions or the consistency or inconsistency of his writings. Wesley was neither a "Mr. Facing-bothways" in the Bunyan tradition, nor an indifferent (much less superficial) theologian. At the same time, he had not the luxury of time nor the inclination of mind to spend time in his study developing a thoroughly consistent theological system. He faced issues as they arose, in the midst of an active ministry to the poor. His theology was hammered out on the anvil of controversy. He was, you might say, a man fighting in the trenches, waging his battle for truth (as he saw it) with the enemy wherever it raised its head, countering attacks from left and right as they came. In that context, he often found it necessary to change his stance to face an opponent more effectively, not unlike a swordsman changing his direction and shifting his footing while holding his ground. When defending himself against the left, he appears to be coming from the right; when facing right, he seems to be defending the left. This is an important consideration when we are trying to discover a basic "Wesleyan" theological position; and, when we look at Wesley's controversial writings in this light, we are likely to discover that he was more consistent than many persons have acknowledged. In fact, he was in most cases trying to hold a middle ground, a stance that is characteristic of his theological method.

4) *Wesley embodied ideals and qualities not always easily held together or reconciled.* Part of the enigma of Wesley is characterized by the frequent portrayal of him in such guises as a "radical conservative," a "romantic realist," or a "quiet revolutionary." While these designations seem to be inherently inconsistent, they do speak to the tension and balance that is a basic element of Wesley's life and thought.

Wesley was an educated upper-class Oxford don who spent most of his life working among the poor and disadvantaged. This paradoxical life-style left its mark on the character of many of his activities. He was a champion of the poor, yet a defender of the political establishment that had caused many of their problems. He was a master of expression in several languages, yet strove to express "plain truth for plain people." In his outlook and activities, he attempted to unite, in his brother Charles' words, "the pair so long disjoined, knowledge and vital piety." He combined in his ministry the preaching of the revivalist and the concerns of the social worker. His religious perspective was at the same time evangelical and sacramental. If we fail to keep in mind this tendency to hold seeming opposites together in unity (though not without some internal tension), we will miss one of the significant keys to understanding his life and thought.

The eclectic methodology that underlies much of Wesley's work, both as a controversial writer and as a mediating theologian in the Anglican tradition, entails the holding together of ideas or emphases that appear to come from opposing sides of the religious spectrum. In a given controversy, Wesley at times found himself having to defend or emphasize one side of such a tandem set, often at the apparent expense of the other side. This combination of eclectic and polemical methodologies on Wesley's part has often confused many observers (past and present), especially if they have not seen a particular selection from his writings, containing only one side of Wesley's view, in the larger context of the whole of his life and writings. So we can find, for example, quotations from Wesley that appear to sound a note of advanced liberalism and to play down the importance of theological differences among professed Christians (e.g., "if your heart is as my heart, give me your hand"), and yet in close proximity we find a call for firmness on fundamental doctrines. If one side of this balance is lost, or one side is overemphasized, the wholeness of the basic Wesleyan position is destroyed (even though Wesley can be cited to support either side in an argument). All this is to say that, in trying to recapture the whole John Wesley, we should look at the context in which his writings were produced. We should pay attention to the nature of controversies that gave rise to certain writings as well as remember that his writings can be best understood when viewed in the light of both the variety of sources that provide the tapestry upon which his developing thought was woven, and the rather massive body of his own works, written over a long lifetime. This observation leads us to a final consideration.

5) *Wesley's life and thought are marked by growth and change.* The story is told of a professor who once lectured on Wesley to a group of inquisitive youngsters. At the conclusion of his presentation, one of the questions from his young audience was, "How old was Wesley?" The professor thought for a moment before replying, "Well, you see, he was different ages at different times." A silly comment, perhaps, but it points to a truism that is frequently overlooked—Wesley grew and changed and developed. We like to define Wesley's life and thought in categorical and simplistic statements that overlook the obvious fact that Wesley was at one time young, that he matured, that he grew old. His life spanned nearly the whole of the eighteenth century. It is quite natural that he developed and changed in many ways (as did the environment around him). His activities, his outlooks, his habits, his thoughts do certainly exhibit some continuity throughout his life; but historians and biographers have had a tendency to see more continuity than is warranted in some areas while overlooking it in others. Wesley's sermons, especially the forty-four "standard" ones, are often treated as a unified body of doctrine, as though they can somehow define the whole of his thought from beginning to end. They are treated, moreover, as though they can stand apart from any historical context or any other sermons he may have written earlier or later. The underlying assumption seems to be that he had all his worthwhile thoughts between the ages of thirty-five and sixty, and that everything before and after was either consistent with those views or otherwise inconsequential. We must be careful to recognize that Wesley developed many of his lifelong habits and ideas as a young man, and also that many of his finest and most mature reflections are exhibited in his writings from the three decades of his life after age sixty.

The problem of analyzing Wesley's development is not simply confined to distinguishing areas of change that are often overlooked. Another tendency to be guarded against is that of seeing changes themselves as being more pervasive and definitive than they might in fact have been. In the most radical of changes there are usually significant threads of continuity. In Wesley's case, the traditional division of his life into two time periods—before and after "Aldersgate"—distorts the picture of his spiritual development and in some ways clouds the actual significance of that crucial event in his life. There has been a tendency in some circles to view the early Wesley as being less than fully Christian and not worth studying, while assuming that the transformation of his evangelical experience of 1738 resulted in a totally new person who was thenceforth consistently persuasive and successful in both his proclamation and experience of the gospel (and therefore more important and worthy of study, if not emulation).

We must recognize, then, that there is more *continuity* between the young Wesley and the mature Wesley than is generally recognized. At the same time we must realize that there is also more *difference* between the mature Wesley and the elderly Wesley than has usually been noticed. The early Wesley, often portrayed as "unenlightened" and "unconverted," exhibits a mind and spirit that provided the foundation and framework for many of his later thoughts and activities. A simple indication of this is the fact that many of the works quoted in his later sermons come from his reading list as a student and tutor at Oxford. On the other hand, some of Wesley's best reflective writing came after his sixtieth birthday, after the last of the "standard" sermons had been written. When he finally published a collected edition of his works in the 1770s, he incorporated nine of these later sermons into the earlier group (bringing the total to fifty-three). Some of these new sermons modified or extended the ideas expressed in the earlier writings. A decade later, he produced yet another edition of his sermons, more than doubling the number of his published sermons by including dozens written after his seventy-fifth birthday. These and other writings from Wesley's later years deserve more attention than they usually receive.

One pitfall that must be avoided in the attempt to discern the nature and character of Wesley's development is, again, the temptation to generalize on the basis of Wesley's own comments, taken out of context. He does occasionally express a view of his own growth and development that he himself later challenges. This is most noticeable in his *Journal* comments regarding the state of his soul in the 1730s. These comments were first published in the 1740s, and then later qualified in the 1770s. We must assume that what he believed about himself at any given time is true for him at that time. Later reflections upon his earlier conditions must be accepted for what they are, an indication of his self-awareness at a later time. That is to say, neither one is "right" or "wrong" absolutely, but simply must be understood in the historical context of his own developing self-consciousness. Thus in 1725, he thought he was a Christian; for a while after 1738, he thought he had not truly been a Christian in 1725; by the 1770s, he was willing to admit that perhaps his middle views were wrong, and that he could understand himself as having been in some real sense a Christian in 1725.

Each of these five considerations listed above, then, emphasizes the necessity to view Wesley in the light of the *whole* of his life and thought. The private man must be considered along with the public; his defense must be placed alongside the attack; his apparent leanings in any given direction must be measured against his penchant for a mediating balance; his views from any given period must stand the test of his own changing mind. We must look for the elusive John Wesley in the context of the many events and controversies that shaped his mind and spirit from beginning to end. And we must look at the sources with a critical eye, noting whether they are early or late, friendly or antagonistic, public or private, exaggerated or simplistic, firsthand or secondary accounts. As a result of this approach, the object of our quest, John Wesley, though still elusive, will in the end be more understandable and believable as a human being.

Twice-Told Tales: Two Centuries of Wesley Studies

Many biographies of Wesley are still repeating favorite, time-worn images of the man that are as inadequate (if not inaccurate) today as they were two hundred years ago. A handful of stock answers have developed over the years to respond to a short list of standard questions that seem to fascinate most authors who join the attempt to portray Wesley for their generation. The questions are usually phrased something like this:

Was Wesley's Aldersgate experience a "conversion"?

Did his influence prevent a revolution in eighteenth-century England?

Did a mother-fixation cause problems in his developing relationships with other women?

Did he intend to start a new denomination?

Was he fascinated more by organizational schemes than theological consistency?

These questions cry for a yes or no answer, and traditional arguments abound to support both sides. If the truth were known, in most cases *both* answers would likely be possible, and *neither* by itself would be fully appropriate.

Part of the problem is that in many cases the wrong questions are being asked, and therefore the answers often do not focus on the most significant issues. It has been said that historians have an uncanny penchant for answering questions that nobody is asking. Many Wesley biographies demonstrate a slight variant of this tendency, answering questions that are being asked, to be sure, but that are off the mark or poorly phrased. As an example, the first question above (about Aldersgate) certainly can be answered yes if one is to believe Wesley's own testimony in the weeks and months immediately following the event. It can also be answered no if one is to believe Wesley's own later alteration of his earlier opinion. A question that would serve us better in trying to understand the significance of this event in Wesley's life would be, What part did Wesley's

Aldersgate experience have in his own developing self-perception (at the time and later) and in his lifelong theological and spiritual development? Asking the question this way begins to point us toward areas of investigation that demand no less interpretation, but are less prone to invite an immediate division into polemical parties or opposing sides, which in the end would have only limited usefulness in moving us toward a more adequate view of Wesley. It is of little value to continue to ask these same questions and then to pick one or another of the old (or even new) stereotypes that argue a poor answer to a bad question.

One reason that traditional questions about Wesley have been the focus of concern over the last two centuries is that most of the major studies of Wesley have been written by persons who would claim to be in the Wesleyan tradition (though not necessarily with a "Methodist" affiliation). Not that the followers of Wesley are somehow inherently incapable of producing good work—fortunately there are many good books and articles around that disprove such an assumption. There has been a tendency, however, for Wesleyans (including Methodists) of various persuasions to "use" Wesley to prove their own point of view or to substantiate the perspective of their own particular branch of the developing, increasingly fragmented heritage. Any one of several brands of "Wesleyanism" can be identified by their use of a predictable litany of certain answers to the time-worn list of standard questions.

A similar tendency toward interpretive categorization can be seen in writings that come out of other, transdenominational groupings. "Evangelicals" have portrayed a Wesley who looks much like a frontier revivalist; the "social gospel" folk like to see Wesley the philanthropist and social worker; the "holiness" faction stresses the centrality of his doctrine of sanctification; the "ecumenical" types emphasize his catholic spirit; the "fundamentalists" build upon a defined package of his essential doctrines—each of these, and others besides, editing Wesley carefully so as to fit into a mold that is, not surprisingly, identical to their own. Most of these interpretive positions tell us something important about Wesley, but fall short of seeing the larger scope of his life and thought.

In the face of all this, many Methodists began to disregard Wesley some time ago, and most non-Methodists have seen little reason to change their long-standing tendency to ignore him. The hagiographical tinfoil that the hero cults put around Wesley's image certainly was not designed to attract serious scholars, and the variety of sectarian claims for a "true Wesleyan" position often discouraged nearly all but the partisans of one side or another. The interpretive writings of specialists provided help only within limited areas of interest.

Writings focused on Wesley by non-Methodists generally decreased in number over the years until very recently. The polemical attacks died out early in the nineteenth century, and subsequent less polemical works were more often than not politely ignored by the majority of readers (for the large part, Methodists) or even treated with a hint of disdain (to think that an "outsider" would presume to understand "their" man!). This trend began to change early in this century as the ecumenical movement began to gain momentum, and the interest in Wesley by non-Methodists has been sustained and promoted by the move toward more interdisciplinary studies in the last twenty years. Students and scholars in many fields are increasingly attracted to the richness and variety of motifs wrapped together in this one fascinating eighteenth-century person.

Unfortunately, in the face of this renewed interest in Wesley's life and thought both from inside and outside the Methodist traditions, we stand in dire need of basic resources such as a fully adequate biographical study and a critical, annotated edition of his works. While not a biography, and certainly short of definitive, this study is intended to introduce the reader to the problems of and procedures for discovering John Wesley—to introduce the novice to and remind the expert of the many possibilities as well as the pitfalls that await persons trying to understand John Wesley. Through looking at a variety of selections of writings by Wesley himself, by his contemporaries, and by successive generations of historians and biographers, we will be able to see the origin of many of the time-worn stereotypes and legends, as well as the places where some revisions need to be made. And through it all we will recognize and be reminded that Wesley is a fascinatingly complex and elusive (though not incomprehensible) eighteenth-century personality.

CHAPTER 1

A SON OF EPWORTH

Strange as it may seem, Samuel Wesley, rector of Epworth and *ex officio* keeper of the parish records, had trouble keeping track of how many children had been born of Susanna, his wife. John Wesley was either the thirteenth or fourteenth; no one is quite sure. We do know that John was, up to the point of his birth on June 17, 1703, only the seventh child in the household to survive the first year of life. At least one baby girl, Susanna, and five boys had already died in infancy. Their names were sometimes used again; the next girl born after Susanna was given the same name.

John was the third boy to be christened with that name. The first John had died shortly after birth in 1699 along with a twin, Benjamin. The second, also a twin (with Anne), had been named John Benjamin, but died at seven months of age, less than eighteen months before the birth of our John (called "Jacky") in 1703.

As the years passed, the parents seem to have confused the circumstances surrounding the naming of these children, giving rise to a family tradition that it was the *surviving* John who had a middle name. Later in the century, one of John Wesley's preachers heard him repeat this tradition and recorded it in an early published history of Methodism: "I have heard him say, that he was baptized by the name of John

Benjamin; that his mother had buried two sons, one called John, and the other Benjamin, and that she united their names in him." The author, Jonathan Crowther, went on to say, "But he never made use of the second name."

The tradition of Wesley's middle name is manifestly false and can be so proved from copies of baptismal records preserved in Samuel Wesley's own hand! That John himself perpetuated such a tradition is perhaps simply an indication of his tendency toward credulity in such matters. But that this and many other such traditions still persist and are repeated in many of the most recent biographies of Wesley is an early warning of the problems that, at every turn, confront the person interested in trying to discover the elusive John Wesley.

We rely on very slim evidence for information about the early life of John Wesley. Two events, however, did etch themselves on his mind—a fire that devastated his home when he was only five years old, and the appearances of a poltergeist that haunted the rectory for a time while John was away at grammar school. These are both well documented in the writings of the Wesley family and seem to have been firmly fastened in John's self-consciousness.

A Brand Plucked out of the Burning

Young John was rescued from the rectory fire "by almost a miracle," as his father reported in a letter at the time. His mother's account was slightly less exuberant in many respects, and Wesley later published it, highly edited and abridged, along with some other letters in the first issue of his monthly *Arminian Magazine* in 1778. He prefaced the collection of letters with a note saying that he hoped "what has been of use to ourselves, may be of use to others also." The letter that Susanna had written describing the rectory fire to a neighboring clergyman, Joseph Hoole, was introduced by John to his readers as "an account of a very remarkable Providence," adding: "But it is imperfect with regard to me. That part none but I myself can supply."

In this published version, John made some alterations in Susanna's account and paraphrased or abridged much of the story.

On Wednesday night, February the ninth [1709], between the hours of eleven and twelve, some sparks fell from the roof of our house, upon one of the children's (Hetty's) feet. She immediately ran to our chamber and called us. Mr. Wesley, hearing a cry of "Fire" in the street, started up (as I was very ill, he lay in a separate room from me), and opening his door, found the fire was in his own house. He immediately came to my room and bid me and my two eldest daughters rise quickly and shift for ourselves. Then he ran and burst open the nursery door and called to the maid to bring out the children. The two little ones lay in the bed with her; the three others, in another bed. She snatched up the youngest and bid the rest follow, which the three elder did. When we were got into the hall and were surrounded with flames, Mr. Wesley found he had left the keys of the door above stairs. He ran up and recovered them, a minute before the staircase took fire. When we opened the street door, the strong northeast wind drove the flames in with such violence that none could stand against them. But some of our children got out through the windows, the rest through a little door into the garden. I was not in a condition to climb up to the windows; neither could I get to the garden door. I endeavoured three times to force my passage through the street door, but was as often beat back by the fury of the flames. In this distress, I besought our blessed Saviour for help and then waded through the fire, naked as I was, which did me no farther harm than a little scorching my hands and my face.

When Mr. Wesley had seen the other children safe, he heard the child in the nursery cry. He attempted to go up the stairs, but they were all on fire and would not bear his weight. Finding it impossible to give any help, he kneeled down in the hall and recommended the soul of the child to God.

[At this point, Wesley broke off his mother's account and continued with his own description of the manner by which he was rescued:]

I believe it was just at that time I waked, for I did not cry, as they imagined, unless it was afterwards. I remember all the circumstances as distinctly as though it were but yesterday. Seeing the room was very light, I called to the maid to take me up. But none answering, I put my head out of the [bed] curtains and saw streaks of fire on the top of the room. I got up and ran to the door but could get no farther, all the floor beyond it being in a blaze. I then climbed up on a chest which stood near the window. One in the yard saw me and proposed running to fetch a ladder. Another answered, "There will not be time; but I have thought of another expedient. Here I will fix myself against the wall; lift a light man and set him on my shoulders." They did so, and he took me out of the window. Just then the whole roof fell, but it fell inward, or we had all been crushed at once. When they brought me into the house where my father was, he cried out, "Come, neighbours! Let us kneel down! Let us give thanks to God! He has given me all eight children; let the house go, I am rich enough!". . . .

A Child of Destiny

Both narratives of the fire, by John and Susanna, emphasize the providential deliverance of *all* the children. At some point, however, the focus of the remembered story began to center on John who, by at least 1737, adopted for himself the phrase from the Old Testament prophets, "a brand plucked out of the burning" [cf. Amos 4:11, Zech. 3:2]. This image he later included in a self-composed epitaph, written in 1753 when he thought death was imminent. It also formed the caption to a small vignette of the rectory fire placed at the bottom of an early portrait of Wesley circulated at mid-century. This biblical image, taken out of its context, became part of the Wesley legend, not only as an indication of his providential delivery from the fire but also as a divine designation of some extraordinary destiny for him (as with Moses, Jesus, Luther, et al.). After Wesley's death, his biographers made this connection quite readily, using a comment from a prayer in Susanna's meditational journal of 1711 as a key element of their interpretation ("I do intend to be more particularly careful of

JOHN WESLEY, M.A.
Fellow of Lincoln College, Oxford

The embellishments on this 1742 engraving of the young Mr. Wesley by George Vertue (1684–1756) include a vignette depicting Wesley's escape from the Epworth rectory fire as "a brand plucked out of the fire," an image that became fixed in Wesley's self-consciousness (see below, pages 42, 82, 96, 196).

the soul of this child, that thou hast so mercifully provided for, than ever I have been").

This part of the Wesley legend, however, was firmly fixed in the popular imagination long before the biographers made any artificial connection by such prooftexting. Even Wesley's own denials of any special self-consciousness on his part (much less his mother's) did little to squelch an image that had already been implicitly nurtured by the tone as well as the content of some of his own writings, such as his *Journal.* His own denials may even have helped perpetuate and strengthen the image. One particularly firm and pointed disclaimer was published by Wesley in response to a brief review by Samuel Badcock, in the *Gentleman's Magazine* of 1784, of John Nichols' *Bibliotheca Topographica Britannica* (XX), which contained a short notice of Wesley. Badcock commented particularly on the rectory fire and its implications:

This extraordinary incident explains a certain device in some of the earlier prints of John Wesley, viz. a *house in flames,* with this motto from the prophet, "Is he not a brand plucked out of the burning?" Many have supposed this device to be merely *emblematical* of his spiritual deliverance. But from this circumstance you must be convinced that it hath a *primary* as well as a *secondary* meaning. It is *real* as well as *allusive*—this fire happened when John was about six years old. . . . He had early a very strong impression (like Count Zinzendorf) of his designation to some extraordinary work. This impression received additional force from some domestic incidents, all which his active fancy turned to his own account. His wonderful preservation, already noticed, naturally tended to cherish the idea of his being designed by Providence to accomplish some purpose or other that was out of the ordinary course of human events.

Wesley's reply, published in the next volume of the *Gentleman's Magazine* (and reprinted for his own readers in the *Arminian Magazine*), attempts to clear up some points on which he says Badcock and the public had been "misinformed." In two paragraphs, Wesley gives an outline of his early life in an attempt to discount any claims to a self-conscious special destiny:

> I was born in June 1703 and was between six and seven years old [*sic*] when I was left alone in my father's house, being then all in flames, till I was taken out of the nursery window by a man strangely standing on the shoulders of another. Those words in the picture, "Is not this a brand plucked out of the burning?" chiefly allude to this.

> "He had early a very strong impression of his designation to some extraordinary work [quoting Badcock]." Indeed not I; I never said so. I am guiltless in this matter. The strongest impression I had till I was three or four and twenty was, *Inter sylvas Academi quaerere verum* [to seek for truth in the groves of Academe], and afterwards (while I was my father's curate), to save my own soul and those that heard me. When I returned to Oxford [in 1729], it was my full resolve to live and die there, the reasons for which I gave in a long letter to my father, since printed in one of my Journals. In this purpose I continued till Dr. Burton, one of the trustees for Georgia, pressed me to go over with General Oglethorpe (who is still alive and well knows the whole transaction) in order to preach to the Indians. With great difficulty I was prevailed upon to go and spent upwards of two years abroad. At my return, I was more than ever determined to lay my bones at Oxford. But I was insensibly led, without any previous plan or design, to preach first in many of the churches in London, then in more public places; afterwards in Bristol, Kingswood, Newcastle, and throughout Great Britain and Ireland. Therefore all that Mr. Badcock adds, of the incidents that "gave additional force" to an impression that never existed, is very ingenious, yet is in truth a castle in the air.

Such "castles in the air," however, capture the imagination and are the stuff of which legends are made, legends that survive long after the history is forgotten.

A Collector of Ghost-lore

A second "domestic incident" mentioned by Badcock as "giving additional force" to Wesley's self-consciousness was the strange noises that disrupted the Epworth rectory in 1716–17:

There were some strange *phaenomena* perceived at the parsonage at Epworth and some uncommon noises heard there from time to time, which he was very curious in examining into and very particular in relating. I have little doubt but that he considered himself as the chief object of this *wonderful* visitation. Indeed, Samuel Wesley's credulity was in some degree affected by it; since he collected all the evidences that tended to confirm the story and arranged them with scrupulous exactness in a MS consisting of several sheets, and which is still in being. I know not what became of the Ghost of Epworth, unless, considered as a prelude to the *noise* Mr. John Wesley made on a more ample stage, it ceased to speak when he began to act.

Wesley's reply to Badcock completely ignored this reference to the ghost of Epworth, no doubt in large part because of its nasty conclusion, but also perhaps because Wesley could not honestly deny his long-standing and lively interest in supernatural phenomena. In August 1726, John had in fact transcribed his father's collected account of the "disturbances" of 1716–17. During the following fortnight he also collected further evidence for himself in the form of recollections from other family members and friends who had heard "Old Jeffrey" (as sister Emily had named the ghost). It is perhaps no strange coincidence that during the very period he was gathering these stories, John himself experienced two similarly strange happenings in the rectory which he recorded in his diary:

Tuesday morning, September 13 [1726], I waked a little before two o'clock and could not go to sleep again. About a quarter after two, the chamber door opened and clapped to again twice, loud and distinctly. Tory [the dog], who was in bed, growled and barked all the time. On Wednesday, as my brother and I were trying to catch a chicken in the same room about twelve o'clock, I stayed at the door to catch it, if it came that way. While I was standing about a yard from it, and looking at it, the door which made wide open moved slowly to. I opened it and looked, but no one beside us two was above stairs.

Wesley's fascination with haunted houses, witches, and other objects of local folklore was firmly grounded in his early experiences in the rural hinterlands of Epworth, isolated as it was on the Isle of Axholme. His firsthand acquaintance with country superstitions may indeed have played a major role in helping him bridge the "culture gap" between his Oxford-educated outlook and the rather primitive world view of many of the folk throughout the kingdom to whom he later ministered.

Perhaps it was this point of contact that he was cultivating when he published in the 1784 *Arminian Magazine* "An Account of the Disturbances in My Father's House." As early as 1730, he had broadcast his father's account of the noises, reading it to the prisoners in the Oxford Castle. But for his readers fifty years later, he put together his own version of the story. Although based on the testimonies he had taken earlier, the sequence of events he outlines is far from accurate, specific incidents being sometimes combined or altered to make the story flow better. The narrative, however, does provide the essential elements of the story, as remolded by Wesley's memory and editorial pen, while also presenting an interesting glimpse into the daily routine of the Epworth household, as the following selections show.

When I was very young, I heard several letters read, wrote to my elder brother by my father, giving an account of strange disturbances, which were in his house, at Epworth, in Lincoln-shire.

1. When I went down thither, in the year [1726], I carefully enquired into the particulars. I spoke to each of the persons who were then in the house, and took down what each could testify of his or her own knowledge. The sum of which was this.

2. On December 2, 1716, while Robert Brown, my father's servant, was sitting with one of the maids a little before ten at night, in the dining-room which opened into the garden, they both heard one knocking at the door. Robert rose and opened it, but

could see nobody. Quickly it knocked again and groaned. "It is Mr. Turpin," said Robert, "he had the stone and used to groan so." He opened the door again twice or thrice, the knocking being twice or thrice repeated. But still seeing nothing, and being a little startled, they rose and went up to bed. . . .

When he was in bed, he heard as it were the gobbling of a turkey-cock, close to the bedside, and soon after, the sound of one stumbling over his shoes and boots. But there were none there; he had left them below.

3. The next day, he and the maid related these things to the other maid, who laughed heartily, and said, "What a couple of fools are *you*? I defy anything to fright *me*." After churning in the evening, she put the butter in the tray, and had no sooner carried it into the dairy, than she heard a knocking on the shelf where pancheons of milk stood, first above the shelf, then below. She took the candle and searched both above and below; but being able to find nothing, threw down butter, tray and all, and ran away for life.

4. The next evening between five and six o'clock my sister Molly, then about twenty years of age, sitting in the dining-room, reading, heard as if it were the door that led into the hall open, and a person walking in, that seemed to have on a silk nightgown, rustling and trailing along. It seemed to walk round her, then to the door, then round again; but she could see nothing. She thought, "It signifies nothing to run away, for whatever it is, it can run faster than me." So she rose, put her book under her arm, and walked slowly away.

5. After supper, she was sitting with my sister Suky (about a year older than her) in one of the chambers, and telling her what had happened, she quite made light of it, telling her, "I wonder you are so easily frighted; I would fain see what would fright *me*." Presently a knocking began under the table. She took the candle and looked, but could find nothing. Then the iron casement began to clatter, and the lid of a warming-pan. Next the latch of the door moved up and down without ceasing. She started up, leaped into the bed without undressing, pulled the bedclothes over her head, and never ventured to look up till next morning. . . .

8. The next morning my sister telling my mother what had happened, she said, "If I hear anything myself, I shall know how to

judge." Soon after, [Emily] begged her [mother] to come into the nursery. She did, and heard in the corner of the room, as it were the violent rocking of a cradle; but no cradle had been there for some years. She was convinced it was preternatural, and earnestly prayed it might not disturb her in her own chamber at the hours of retirement. And it never did.

She now thought it was proper to tell my father. But he was extremely angry, and said, "Suky, I am ashamed of you. These boys and girls fright one another; but you are a woman of sense, and should know better. Let me hear of it no more."

At six in the evening, he had family prayers as usual. When he began the prayer for the king, a knocking began all round the room, and a thundering knock attended the *Amen*. The same was heard from this time every morning and evening while the prayer for the king was repeated.

As both my father and mother are now at rest, and incapable of being pained thereby, I think it my duty to furnish the serious reader with a key to this circumstance. The year before King William died, my father observed my mother did not say "Amen" to the Prayer for the king. She said she could not, for she did not believe the Prince of Orange was king. He vowed he would never cohabit with her till she did. He then took his horse and rode away, nor did she hear anything of him for a twelvemonth. He then came back and lived with her as before. But I fear his vow was not forgotten before God.

9. Being informed that Mr. Hoole, the Vicar of Haxey (an eminently pious and sensible man) could give me some farther information, I walked over to him. He said, "Robert Brown came over to me, and told me, your father desired my company. When I came he gave me an account of all that had happened, particularly the knocking during family prayer. But that evening (to my great satisfaction) we had no knocking at all. But between nine and ten, a servant came in and said, Old Jeffries is coming (that was the name of one that died in the house) for I hear the signal. This they informed me was heard every night about a quarter before ten. It was toward the top of the house on the outside, at the northeast corner, resembling a loud creaking of a saw, or rather that of a windmill when the body of it is turned about in order to shift the sails to the wind. We then heard a knocking over our heads, and

Mr. Wesley catching up a candle, said, Come, Sir, now you shall hear for yourself. We went upstairs; he with much hope and I (to say the truth) with much fear. When we came into the nursery, it was knocking in the next room; when we were there, it was knocking in the nursery. And there it continued to knock, though we came in, particularly at the head of the bed (which was of wood) in which Miss Hetty and two of her younger sisters lay. Mr. Wesley observing that they were much affected though asleep, sweating and trembling exceedingly, was very angry, and pulling out a pistol, was going to fire at the place from whence the sound came. But I catched him by the arm and said, Sir, you are convinced this is something preternatural. If so, you cannot hurt *it*, but you give it power to hurt *you*. He then went close to the place and said sternly, 'Thou deaf and dumb devil, why dost thou fright these children that cannot answer for themselves? Come to *me* in my study, that am a man?' Instantly it knocked *his* knock (the particular knock which he always used at the gate [1-23456-7]) as if it would shiver the board in pieces, and we heard nothing more that night."

10. Till this time, my father had never heard the least disturbance in his study. But the next evening, as he attempted to go into his study (of which none had any key but himself) when he opened the door, it was thrust back with such violence as had like to have thrown him down. However, he thrust the door open and went in. Presently there was knocking first on one side, then on the other; and after a time, in the next room, wherein my sister Nancy was. He went into that room, and (the noise continuing) adjured it to speak, but in vain. He then said, "These spirits love darkness; put out the candle and perhaps it will speak." She did so, and he repeated his adjuration, but still there was only knocking and no articulate sound. Upon this he said, "Nancy, two Christians are an over-match for the devil. Go all of you downstairs; it may be, when I am alone, he will have courage to speak." When she was gone, a thought came in and he said, "If thou art the spirit of my son Samuel, I pray, knock three knocks and no more." Immediately all was silence, and there was no more knocking at all that night. . . .

13. A few nights after, my father and mother were just gone to bed and the candle was not taken away, when they heard three

blows, and a second, and a third three, as it were with a large oaken staff struck upon a chest which stood by the bedside. My father immediately arose, put on his nightgown, and hearing great noises below, took the candle and went down. My mother walked by his side. As they went down the broad stairs, they heard as if a vessel full of silver was poured upon my mother's breast and ran jingling down to her feet. Quickly after there was a sound as if a large iron ball was thrown among many bottles under the stairs. But nothing was hurt. Soon after our large mastiff dog came and ran to shelter himself between them. While the disturbances continued, he used to bark and leap, and snap on one side and the other, and that frequently, before any person in the room heard any noise at all. But after two or three days, he used to tremble and creep away before the noise began. And by this, the family knew it was at hand; nor did the observation ever fail. . . .

14. Several gentlemen and clergymen now earnestly advised my father to quit the house. But he constantly answered, "No; let the devil flee from *me*; I will never flee from the devil." But he wrote to my eldest brother at London, to come down. He was preparing so to do, when another letter came, informing him the disturbances were over, after they had continued (the latter part of the time, day and night) from the second of December to the end of January.

CHAPTER 2

THE OXFORD DON

Wesley finished his preliminary schooling at Charterhouse in London in 1720 and went up to Christ Church, Oxford, to do his collegiate studies. He graduated as a bachelor of arts in 1724 and remained at Oxford to continue studies for a master of arts degree. His desire to pursue the scholarly life as a fellow and tutor at the University led him to seek ordination, prerequisite for such a position. His father reassured him that there was "no harm" in such a rationale for entering into Orders, but suggested that "a desire and intention to lead a stricter life" was a better reason. His mother concurred, pleased by the "alteration of [his] temper," and sent him a few lines of advice in February 1725: "Dear Jacky, I heartily wish you would now enter upon a serious examination of yourself, that you may know whether you have a reasonable hope of salvation. . . . I approve the disposition of your mind; I think this season of Lent the most proper for your preparation for Orders."

Within days of receiving the encouragement from his parents, John began listing rules and resolutions in a small notebook that would become his daily diary. His reading that Lenten season set him on a course of self-examination that was designed to promote "holy living." His progress was to be both encouraged and measured by the strict "care of time" entailed in keeping a diary. Wesley continued to keep a private daily diary for the rest of his life. The first few volumes, covering ten years (as yet unpublished), provide an unmatched resource for discovering details about Wesley's life at Oxford.

The following selections, chosen from his private writings (diaries and letters), illustrate a small portion of the variety of Wesley's personal concerns and interests during the decade that saw "the first rise of Methodism" at Oxford. The grand theme of holy living had begun to set the direction of his life, even though the specific agenda of activities and his theological underpinnings would continue to experience some shifts though the coming years. He was increasingly obsessed with a desire for some clear sense of assurance that his approach and method of Christian living would provide adequate grounds for his hope of salvation.

The Careful Diarist

Wesley's diary entries (even the developing format) show an increasingly introspective manner, which is perhaps best characterized as "meditative piety." The temptations that beset him are transparent, not only in his explicit comments but also implicitly in his lists of resolutions and rules, beginning with the very first in 1725:

[Good] Friday, March 26, 1725. I found a great many unclean thoughts arising in Chapel, and discovered these temptations to it:
  a. Too much addicting myself to light behaviour at all times;
  b. Listening too much to idle talk, and reading vain plays and books;
  c. Idleness; and lastly
  [d] Want of due consideration in whose presence I am.
From which I perceive it is necessary
  a. To labour for a grave and modest carriage;
  b. To avoid vain and light company; and
  c. To entertain awful apprehensions of the presence of God;
  d. To avoid idleness, freedom with women, and high-seasoned meats;

e. To resist the very beginnings of lust, not by arguing with, but by thinking no more of it or by immediately going into company; and lastly,

[f] To use frequent and fervent prayer.

Wesley's early diary reveals him participating in activities and exercises typical of the Oxford curriculum: reading basic texts, writing themes *(geneses)*, discussing philosophical, political, and religious questions. The pattern of his study can be seen in a schedule drawn up in the diary just a year after his ordination as a deacon and a few months before standing for his master's degree; the rationale for such can be seen outlined in a subsequent letter to his mother.

Sunday morning: read Divinity, collect, compose.

Afternoon: read Divinity, collect.

Monday (Greek and Latin Classics)

Morning: read Greek poets, Homer; historians, Xenophon.

Afternoon: read Latin poets, Terence; historians, Sallust; Oratory, Tully.

Tuesday (Greek and Latin Classics)

Morning: Terence and Sallust or Tully.

Afternoon: Homer and Xenophon.

Wednesday (Sciences)

Morning: Logic—Aldrich, Wallis, Sanderson.

Afternoon: Ethics—Langbain, More, Eustachius.

Thursday (Languages)

Morning: Hebrew grammar, Psalter.

Afternoon: Arabic grammar.

Friday (Sciences)

Morning: Metaphysicks—LeClerc, Locke, Clark, Jackson.

Afternoon: Physics—Bartholine, Rohoult (per Clark), Robinson's Collection.

Saturday (Oratory and Poetry)

Morning: write sermons and letters or verses.

Afternoon: letters or sermons or verses.

September 24, 1726

[To Susanna, his mother, January 24, 1727]

I am shortly to take my Master's degree. As I shall from that time be less interrupted by business not of my own choosing, I have drawn up for myself a scheme of studies from which I do not intend, for some years at least, to vary. I am perfectly come over to your opinion that there are many truths it is not worthwhile to know. Curiosity indeed might be a sufficient plea for our laying out some time upon them, if we had half a dozen centuries of life to come, but methinks it is great ill-husbandry to spend a considerable part of the small pittance now allowed us in what makes us neither a quick nor a sure return. . . .

The daily entries of Wesley's diary for the first few years are punctuated by weekly periods of self-examination listing his sins and shortcomings. Anger, lying, lack of devotion, immoderate play or sleep—these and many other failings are noted fairly regularly (with "idleness" the most common) as indicators that all the virtues are not yet firmly implanted in his soul. Holidays provided something of a change of pace in all this, and the diary records many visits with friends in the Cotswold hills, especially the Kirkhams of Stanton, whose daughters Betty ("Athenais") and Sally ("Varanese") were attracted to Wesley. The selections below display some of the wide range of interests that Wesley had developed at this time as well as the emotional ties that seemed to distract him at times from his professed religious aspirations. The first selection is a marginal note that reveals his interest in developing a genteel style in his social graces.

A Step and a Sink with the other foot
  First, Let the Sink be twice as long as the Step;
  Secondly, Rise very slow;
  Thirdly, Walk slowly into a room until your bow;
  Fourthly, Let your hind foot never move; your hindmost always bends;
  Fifth, Walk a little faster for a lady; first salute her, then bow and hand her to a chair.

Saturday, October 8, 1726. Rode to Stanton. . . . Walked with Nancy to Buckland. Supped there. A fine Aurora Borealis, first in the north, then northwest and northeast, then all round, etc; all the rays terminating near the zenith, rather northwards; appearing by turns of all colours, chiefly red or brick colour; at the height at 8 but very visible at 12; lighted home by it.

Friday, October 14. . . . Walked to Varanese and Betty's; sat with them on the hill an hour. "My sister and I were reflecting as we came hither whether, if we were to die immediately, the action we were upon would give us any pain; and we both agreed that in such a circumstance this design would give us much more pleasure than uneasiness"—Varanese. "You make me less complaisant than I was before, for methinks 'tis almost a sin to prostitute those expressions of tenderness to others which I have at any time applied to you. I can't think it expedient, nor indeed lawful, to break off that acquaintance which is one of the strongest incentives I have to Virtue"—Varanese. . . .

Sunday, October 16. Read prayers twice and preached at Stanton. . . . Walked to Horrel [Hill], sat down an hour with Varanese and Betty. I told them, in spite of the wise maxims of our sex, I was not ashamed to say I loved them sincerely. Varanese replied they were not behindhand with me and that she loved me more than all mankind except her father and her husband, and believed Betty did so too, though a maid must not say too much. At night Betty sat with me again. I told her I desired just the same freedom with her as with my sisters. She told me I had it; goodnight brother at eleven.

Monday, October 17. . . . Varanese and Betty said they would walk with me; walked near two hours. . . . "I would certainly acquit you if my husband should ever resent our freedom, which I am satisfied he never will. Such an accident as this would make it necessary to restrain in some measure the appearance of the esteem I have for you; but the esteem itself, as it is grounded on reason and virtue, and entirely agreeable to both, no circumstance of life shall ever make me alter"—Varanese. . . . Sat with Varanese and Betty till eleven. Leaned on Varanese' breast and kept both her hands within mine. She said very many obliging things. Betty looked tenderly. Thank God; long-suffering. . . .

Friday, December 23. At Stanton; rose at nine; thought what I should talk of; with Betty and Varanese; . . . talk of reason in brutes; how flies and fishes respire; of Miss Tooker, she was noted for good humour ever since she was two years old. At "Take care of thyself, Gentle Yahoo," Betty burst out a-crying; . . . till five with Betty in the kitchen; grave, then merry; wished she had been a man for my sake.

Monday, December 26. . . . Played at cards, lost; much company; talk of sheep and price of corn; read the rest of *Ambitious Stepmother* to Miss Tooker. She commends Mr. Hutchins much for telling her her faults. . . .

Thursday, December 29. Read *Henry IV*; . . . discussed with Mrs. Chapone [Varanese] of the use of astronomy, particularly of comets; why physicians [are] commonly atheists, inured to sickness and death; played at Pope Joan till twelve, won; talk with Varanese till one; of the use of languages, particularly Arabic—how should that be so elegant when the speakers of it for the most part have been so unpolished.

Friday, December 30. Rose at eight, read part of *Way of the World*; . . . played at Ombre till nine; went into kitchen for Athenais, burst into tears at my saying, "how prettily shall we reflect on our past lives thirty or forty years hence?" Said she would tell me then why she would never marry. I told her what [her brother] said of it! She was a little piqued; said I used artifice to get a secret out of her. . . .

Monday, January 9. . . . With Varanese in little parlour; said she always thought she had a vast many things to say to me when I was away, but still forgot them when I came. . . . "The greatest pleasures of my life, I freely own, have been owing to friendship; and in the number of my friends there is no one I see, and always shall, in a stronger view than you"—Varanese.

"Primitive Christianity"

Wesley continued these close friendships for several years, accepting the name "Cyrus" from classical literature as part of the social style among this small literary circle (Charles being "Araspes," a friend of Cyrus the Great; Ann Granville,

"Selima"; Mary Granville Pendarves, "Aspasia"; Betty Kirkham, "Athenais"; and Sally Kirkham Chapone, "Varanese"). Wesley's correspondence with Aspasia and Selima, as well as with members of his family, provides not only a picture of events at Oxford but also an expression, at a very pure and untarnished level, of Wesley's concept of his ideal, the true Christian. The personal discipline that such an ideal evoked in the Oxford don's life-style, implicit in the following selections, caused his lady friends occasionally to apply another nickname to Wesley—"Primitive Christianity."

[To Aspasia, February 11, 1731]

Who can be a fitter person than one that knows it by experience to tell me the full force of that glorious rule, "Set your affections on things above, and not on things of the earth"? Is it equivalent to, "Thou shalt love the Lord thy God with all thy heart, soul, and strength"? But what is it to love God? Is not to love anything the same as habitually to delight in it? Is not then the purport of both these injunctions this, that we delight in the Creator more than his creatures? That we take more pleasure in him than in anything he has made? And rejoice in nothing so much as in serving him? That (to take Mr. Pascal's expression) while the generality of men use God and enjoy the world, we on the contrary only use the world while we enjoy God.

[To Susanna, his mother, June 1, 1731]

The point debated was, What is the meaning of being "righteous overmuch," or by the more common phrase, of being too strict in religion? And what danger there was of any of us falling into that extreme.

All the ways of being too righteous or too strict which we could think of were these: either the carrying some one particular virtue to so great a height as to make it clash with some others; or the laying too much stress on the instituted means of grace, to the neglect of the weightier matters of the law; or the multiplying prudential means upon ourselves so far, and binding ourselves to the observance of them so strictly, as to obstruct the end we aimed at by them, either by hindering our advance in heavenly affections in general, or by retarding our progress in some particular virtue. Our opponents seemed to think my brother and I in some danger of being too strict in this last sense, of laying burdens on ourselves too heavy to be borne, and consequently too heavy to be of any use to us.

. . . This is a subject which we would understand with as much accuracy as possible, it being hard to say which is of the worse consequence: the being too strict, the really carrying things too far, the wearying ourselves and spending our strength in burdens that are unnecessary; or the being frightened by those terrible words from what, if not directly necessary, would at least be useful.

[To Aspasia, July 19, 1731]

. . . I was made to be happy; to be happy I must love God; in proportion to my love of whom my happiness must increase. To love God I must be like him, holy as he is holy; which implies both the being pure from vicious and foolish passions and the being confirmed in those virtues and rational affections which God comprises in the word "charity." In order to root those out of my soul and plant these in their stead I must use (1) such means as are ordered by God, (2) such as are recommended by experience and reason.

[To Selima, August 14, 1731]

I have indeed spent many thoughts on the necessity of method to a considerable progress either in knowledge or virtue, and am still persuaded that they who have but a day to live are not wise if they waste a moment, and are therefore concerned to take the shortest way to every point they desire to arrive at.

The method of, or shortest way to, knowledge, seems to be this: (1) to consider what knowledge you desire to attain to; (2) to read no book which does not some way tend to the attainment of that knowledge; (3) to read no book which does tend to the attainment of it unless it be the best in its kind; (4) "to finish one before you begin another," and lastly, to read them all in such an order that every subsequent book may illustrate and confirm the preceding.

The Compulsive Pietist

Wesley's own rigorous style of life during this period can be discovered quite readily by looking at his developing diary, which by 1733 had become an exacting instrument for taking his spiritual pulse.

Part of Wesley's "method" of holy living was to test himself daily (and eventually hourly) by various sets of questions. The primary concerns of these periods of self-examination can be seen in a list of "General Questions" which he began developing in 1730, enlarging and altering the list as he transcribed it into successive notebook diaries. These concerns provided the framework within which he reflected hourly upon his activities, as seen in a sample daily entry, which records not only his activities every hour (conversations, readings, and so forth) but also the resolutions he had either broken or kept, and his temper of devotion, rated on a scale of 1 to 9. Few major personalities in history have left us quite such an exhaustive record of their activities and attitudes.

General Questions

1. Have I prayed with fervor, by myself and at Chapel?
2. Have I used the Collects at 9, 12, and 3? Grace [at meals]?
3. Have I used the Ejaculations seriously, deliberately, and fervently once an hour?
4. Have I at ingress and egress prayed . . . for the virtue of the day?
5. Have I done or said anything without a present or previous perception of its direct or remote tendency to the glory of God?
6. Have I after every pleasure immediately given thanks?
7. Did I in the morning plan the business of the day?
8. Did I in every action consider the duty of the day? Have I been simple and recollect in everything? The signs?
9. Have I been zealous in undertaking and active in doing what good I could?
10. Have I before I visited or was visited prepared and considered what end, what means?
11. Has good will been and appeared the spring of all my actions toward others?
12. Have I conversed with Charles as Aspasia with Selima? Negative, positive?
13. Have I been or seemed angry?

14. Have I thought or spoken unkindly of or to anyone?
15. Have I felt or entertained or seemed to approve any proud, vain, or unchaste thought?
16. Have I been particularly recollect, temperate, and thankful in eating or drinking?

Sunday, March 17, 1734
6 thirteen times, 7 five times.*

	Temper of Devotion	Resolutions Broken	Kept
4 e Dressed. 4.15 Necessary business. 4.30 Called; writ diary; private prayer.	6	6	4/2
5 e Questions; private prayer. 5.45 Fire [lighted].	6		1
6 e Called; began Clemens Romanus; Ingham, religious talk. 6.45 Robson, tea.	6		5/2
7 e Religious talk of diaries. 7.45 Dressed; Grove.	6	6	
8 e Clemens. 8.30 Morning Prayers [each part listed separately].	7		1
9 e Morning Prayers [continued]. 9.20 Writ diary. 9.30 Castle, Morning Prayers.	7		1
10 e Morning Prayers [continued].	7		1
11 e Sermon, spoke to laughers in faith, looked; Sacrament; resolved not try with Morgan.	7	15	
12 e Bible, Hall's, private prayer; Robson and			

	Salmon, dinner, religious talk.	6	6	16
1 e	Pupil; writ diary. 1.50 Laughed at.	6	3/10	
2 e	Sermon; ended *Reasonable Communicant*.	6		
3 e	Grove, meditated.			
4 e	Questions. 4.10 Evening Prayers. 4.50 Examined.	7	5	1
5 e	Private prayer. 5.30 Eagle's, he not [home], religious talk.	6		
6 e	Salmon's, Horn, etc; examined, tea.	6	5/5	16
7 e	Morgan, Nowell, Walker, began St. Clemens.	6		
8 e	Clemens. 8.15 Religious talk, overbore Morgan.	6		
9 e	Writ diary; private prayer; undressed. 9.30.	6	8	

[Notes to diary page]

* Summary of hourly ratings on "temper of devotion" on a scale of 1 to 9 (higher is better).

"e" stands for ejaculatory prayer at the beginning of each hour, a short sentence prayer of praise; the symbol over it (and many other entries, see illustration, p. 61) indicates the "degree of attention" ranging from dead or cold, to fervent or zealous.

The "resolutions broken or kept" are keyed to various lists by number: the whole numbers (1, 5, 6, 15, 16) refer to the list of "General Questions" (page 58 above); the numbers that look like fractions (4/2, 5/2, etc.) refer to a list of "Particular Questions" arranged according to the virtues:

4/2—Mortification and self-denial, question 2: "Have I submitted my will to the will of everyone that opposed it?"

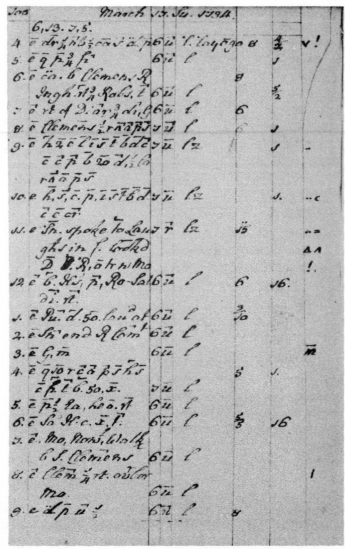

Courtesy, Methodist Archives, Manchester

Entry for March 17, 1734, in Wesley's Oxford Diary (see page 59).

5/2—Resignation and meekness, question 2: "Have I endeavoured to thank Him for whatever has been mine without my choosing?"

5/5—Resignation and meekness, question 5: "Have I been cheerful (without levity), mild and courteous in all I said?"

3/10—Humility, question 10: "Have I omitted justifying myself? Submitted to be thought in the wrong?"

CHAPTER 3

THE OXFORD METHODIST

By mid-1732, Wesley had gathered around him a group of five or six friends who shared his commitment to disciplined Christian living. Toward the end of that year, a seething undercurrent of criticism aimed at Wesley and his small group of seemingly fanatical religious friends came to the surface. Word spread around the university that William Morgan, one of the original members of their group, had died as a result of extreme ascetic practices encouraged by Wesley. The furor that followed, swept on by rumor and the printed word, pushed Wesley into the public eye not only in Oxford and Dublin (Morgan's hometown), but also in London and throughout the British Isles. The attacks put Wesley into a defensive posture that forced him both to explain his ideas and activities to the public, and to satisfy himself about the validity of his vocation as well as his state of salvation.

Apologist for the Oxford Methodists

Two writings by Wesley at that time contain his personal defense and proclaim his theological program. First, a letter to Morgan's father explains the background and rationale of their little society. Second, a sermon preached before the university ("Circumcision of the Heart") proclaims the central thrust of the doctrine that would be the keystone of his theology, Christian perfection. The second writing appears in every collection of Wesley's "standard" sermons. The first, the "Morgan letter," however, became the first instrument of Wesley's defense before officials of the university—he read this letter to the vice-chancellor, the provost of Queen's, the rector of Lincoln, and anyone else who raised questions about the Methodists' activities. During the following months, several copies of the letter were made by Wesley and his friends; the surviving manuscript is in Charles Wesley's handwriting.

The Morgan letter, used by Wesley as the standard defense of Oxford Methodism in 1732, has also become the standard account of its rise and design, even though it does not describe the fullest state of its organization, which emerged only after 1732. The letter's wide circulation, as well as the popularization of the term "Methodist" (apparently first used in 1732), was due in part to an anonymous author who included it nearly verbatim in the first published pamphlet describing Wesley and his group, *The Oxford Methodists* (1733), a not wholly favorable answer to the charges made against the group in a letter to the editor of a London newspaper (see volume 2, page 31). No one, including Wesley, has ever discovered the author of that pamphlet (Wesley retraced his steps with the Morgan letter trying in vain to uncover the "leak"). To set the record straight, Wesley included an unexpurgated copy of the "Morgan letter" as an introductory section to his first published journal extract in 1740, a prominent position it has occupied in nearly every edition since that time. As a result, the descriptions in this letter, somewhat oversimplified as they are, have become etched in the minds of succeeding generations and have provided the basis for many of the stereotypes of the early Wesley and Oxford Methodism.

Oxon, Oct. [19], 1732

Sir,

The occasion of my giving you this trouble is of a very extraordinary nature. On Sunday last I was informed (as no doubt you will be ere long) that my brother and I had killed your son; that the rigorous fasting which he had imposed upon himself, by our advice, had increased his illness and hastened his death. Now though, considering it in itself, "it is a very small thing with me to be judged by man's judgment"; yet as the being thought guilty of so mischievous an imprudence might make me the less able to do the work I came into the world for, I am obliged to clear myself of it by observing to you, as I have done to others, that your son left off fasting about a year and a half since, and that it is not yet half a year since I began to practise it.

I must not let this opportunity slip of doing my part toward giving you a juster notion of some other particulars relating both to him and myself, which have been industriously misrepresented to you. . . .

In November 1729, at which time I came to reside at Oxford, your son, my brother, myself, and one more, agreed to spend three or four evenings in a week together. Our design was to read over the classics, which we had before read in private, on common nights and on Sunday some book in divinity. In the summer following, Mr. Morgan told me he had called at the gaol to see a man who was condemned for killing his wife, and that, from the talk he had with one of the debtors, he verily believed it would do much good if anyone would be at the pains of now and then speaking with them. This he so frequently repeated that on the 24th of August, 1730, my brother and I walked with him to the Castle. We were so well satisfied with our conversation there that we agreed to go thither once or twice a week, which we had not done long, before he desired me to go with him to see a poor woman in the town who was sick. In this employment too, when we came to reflect upon it, we believed it would be worthwhile to spend an hour or two in a week, provided the minister of the parish in which any such person was, were not against it. But that we might not depend wholly on our own judgments, I wrote an account to my father of our whole design, withal begging that he, who had lived seventy years in the world and seen as much of it as most private men have ever done, should advise us whether we had yet gone too far and whether we should now stand still or go forward.

Part of his answer, dated September 21st, 1730, was this:

"And now, as to your own designs and employments, what can I say less of them than, *Valde probo* [I greatly approve], and that I have the highest reason to bless God that he has given me two sons together at Oxford to whom he has given grace and courage to turn the war against the world and the devil, which is the best way to conquer them. They have but one more enemy to combat with, the flesh; which if they take care to subdue by fasting and prayer, there will be no more for them to do but to proceed steadily in the same course and expect 'the crown which fadeth not away.' You have reason to bless God, as I do, that you have so fast a friend as Mr. Morgan, who, I see, in the most difficult service, is ready to break the ice for you. . . . Go on then in God's name in the path to which your Saviour has directed you and that track wherein your father has gone before you! For when I was an undergraduate at Oxford, I visited those in the Castle there and reflect on it with great satisfaction to this day. Walk as prudently as you can, though not fearfully, and my heart and prayers are with you." . . .

> Your most affectionate and joyful father.

In pursuance of these directions, I immediately went to Mr. Gerard, the Bishop of Oxford's chaplain, who was likewise the person that took care of the prisoners when any were condemned to die (at other times they were left to their own care). I proposed to him our design of serving them as far as we could, and my own intention to preach there once a month, if the Bishop approved of it. He much commended our design and said he would answer for the Bishop's approbation, to whom he would take the first opportunity of mentioning it. It was not long before he informed me he had done so, and that his lordship not only gave his permission, but was greatly pleased with the undertaking and hoped it would have the desired success.

Soon after, a gentleman of Merton College, who was one of our little company, which now consisted of five persons, acquainted us that he had been much rallied the day before for being a member of The Holy Club, and that it was become a common topic of mirth at his college, where they had found out several of our customs, to which we were ourselves utter strangers. . . . We still continued to meet together as usual, and to confirm one another as well as we could in our resolutions, to communicate as often as we had opportunity (which is here once a week), and do what service we could do our acquaintance, the prisoners, and two or three poor families in the town. But the outcry daily increasing, that we might show what ground there was for it, we proposed to our friends, or opponents, as we had opportunity, these or the like questions:

I. Whether it does not concern all men of all conditions to imitate Him as much as they can "who went about doing good"? . . .

II. Whether, upon these considerations, we may not try to do good to our acquaintance? Particularly, whether we may not try to convince them of the necessity of being Christians? . . .

III. Whether, upon the considerations above-mentioned, we may not try to do good to those that are hungry, naked, or sick? In particular, whether, if we know any necessitous family, we may not give them a little food, clothes, or physic, as they want? . . .

IV. Lastly, whether, upon the consideration above-mentioned, we may not try to do good to those that are in prison? In particular, whether we may not release such well-disposed persons as remain in prison for small sums? . . .

I do not remember that we met with any person who answered any of these questions in the negative, or who even doubted whether it were not lawful to apply to this use that time and money which we should else have spent in other diversions. But several we met with who increased our little stock of money for the prisoners and the poor by subscribing something quarterly to it, so that the more persons we proposed our designs to, the more we were confirmed in the belief of their innocency and the more determined to pursue them in spite of the ridicule, which increased fast upon us during the winter. However, in the spring I thought it could not be improper to desire farther instructions from those who were wiser and better than ourselves, and accordingly (on May 18th, 1731), I wrote a particular account of all our proceedings to a clergyman of known wisdom and integrity. After having informed him of all the branches of our design as clearly and simply as I could, I next acquainted him with the success it had met with, in the following words:

"Almost as soon as we had made our first attempts this way, some of the men of wit in Christ Church entered the lists against us and, between mirth and anger, made a pretty many reflections upon the Sacramentarians, as they were pleased to call us. Soon after, their allies at Merton changed our title and did us the honour of styling us The Holy Club. But most of them being persons of well-known characters, they had not the good fortune to gain any proselytes from the Sacrament till a gentleman, eminent for learning and well esteemed for piety, joining them, told his nephew that if he dared to go to the weekly communion any longer, he would immediately turn him out of doors. That argument, indeed, had no success; the young gentleman communicated next week, upon which his uncle, having again tried to convince him that he was in the wrong way, by shaking him by the throat to no purpose, changed his method and by mildness prevailed upon him to absent from it the Sunday following, as he has done five Sundays in six ever since. This much delighted our gay opponents, who increased their number apace; especially when, shortly after, one of the seniors of the college having been with the Doctor, upon his return from him sent for two young gentlemen severally who had communicated weekly for some time, and was so successful in his exhortations that for the future they promised to do it only three times in a year. About this time there was a meeting (as one who was present at it informed your son) of several of the officers and seniors of the college, wherein it was consulted what would be the speediest way to stop the progress of enthusiasm in it. The result we know not, only it was soon publicly reported that Dr. Terry and the censors were going to blow up The Godly Club. This was now our common title, though we were sometimes dignified with that of The Enthusiasts, or The Reforming Club.". . .

Your son was now at Holt. However, we continued to meet at our usual times, though our little affairs went on but heavily without him. But at our return from Lincolnshire in September last we had the pleasure of seeing him again, when, though he could not be so active with us as formerly, yet we were exceedingly glad to spend what time we could in talking and reading with him.

It was a little before this time my brother and I were at London when, going into a bookseller's shop (Mr. Rivington's in St. Paul's Churchyard), after some other conversation, he asked us whether we lived in town, and upon our answering, "No, at Oxford,"— "Then, gentlemen," said he, "let me earnestly recommend to your acquaintance a friend I have there, Mr. Clayton, of Brasenose." Of this, having small leisure for contracting new acquaintance, we took no notice for the present. But in the spring following (April 20th), Mr. Clayton meeting me in the street and giving Mr. Rivington's service, I desired his company to my room, and then commenced our acquaintance. At the first opportunity I acquainted him with our whole design, which he immediately and heartily closed with. And not long after, Mr. Morgan having then left Oxford, we fixed two evenings in a week to meet on, partly to talk upon that subject and partly to read something in practical divinity.

The two points whereunto, by the blessing of God and your son's help, we had before attained, we endeavoured to hold fast; I mean, the doing what good we can, and, in order thereto, communicating as often as we have opportunity. To these, by the advice of Mr. Clayton, we have added a third—the observing the fasts of the Church, the general neglect of which we can by no means apprehend to be a lawful excuse for neglecting them. And in the resolution to adhere to these and all things else which we are convinced God requires at our hands, we trust we shall persevere till he calls us to give an account of our stewardship. As for the names of Methodists, Supererogation-men, and so on, with which some of our neighbours are pleased to compliment us, we do not conceive ourselves to be under any obligation to regard them, much less to take them for arguments. "To the law and to the testimony" we appeal, whereby we ought to be judged. If by these it can be proved we are in an error, we will immediately and gladly retract it; if not, we "have not so learned Christ" as to renounce any part of his service, though men should "say all manner of evil against us" with more judgment and as little truth as hitherto. We do, indeed, use all the lawful means we know to prevent "the good which is in us from being evil spoken of." But if the neglect of known duties be the one condition of securing our reputation, why, fare it well; we know whom we have believed, and what we thus lay out He will pay us again. . . .

I have now largely and plainly laid before you the real ground of all the strange outcry you have heard, and am not without hope that by this fairer representation of it than you probably ever received before, both you and the clergyman you formerly mentioned may have a more favourable opinion of a good cause, though under an ill name. Whether you have or no, I shall ever acknowledge my best services to be due to yourself and your family, both for the generous assistance you have given my father and for the invaluable advantages your son has (under God) bestowed on,

Sir, your ever obliged and most obedient servant.

Wesley's letter explaining the nature and design of Methodism at Oxford so successfully convinced Richard Morgan, Sr., of the harmlessness of the Oxford Methodists' practices (and in fact of their value) that the elder Morgan sent his second son and namesake to Oxford under Wesley's care. Richard, Jr., was quickly repelled by Wesley's methods and informed his father of his feelings in no uncertain terms. The father wrote to Wesley. The following excerpt is from Wesley's reply to the father's plea for moderation in dealing with this, his recalcitrant son. Their developing dispute hinges on the question of the nature of religion and the expectations one might impose upon others. The second selection, written by Wesley to his mother, illustrates Wesley's positions and methods with regard to the implicit matter of indoctrination.

[To Richard Morgan, Sr., January 15, 1734]

Why, you say, I am to incite [your son] to "live a sober, virtuous, and religious life." Nay, but first let us agree what religion is. I take religion to be, not the bare saying over so many prayers morning and evening, in public or in private; not anything superadded now and then to a careless or worldly life; but a constant ruling habit of soul; a renewal of our minds in the image of God; a recovery of the divine likeness; a still-increasing conformity of heart and life to the pattern of our most holy Redeemer. But if this be religion, if this be that way to life which our Blessed Lord hath marked out for us, how can anyone, while he keeps close to this way, be charged with running into extremes? . . .

[To Susanna, his mother, August 17, 1733]
. . . I cannot say whether I "rigorously impose any observances on others" till I know what that phrase means. What I do is this. When I am entrusted with a person who is first to understand and practise, and then to teach the law of Christ, I endeavour by an intermixture of reading and conversation to show him what that law is; that is, to renounce all insubordinate love of the world, and to love and obey God with all his strength. When he appears seriously sensible of this I propose to him the means God hath commanded him to use in order to that end; and a week or a month or a year after, as the state of his soul seems to require it, the several prudential means recommended by wise and good men. As to the times, order, measure, and manner wherein these are to be proposed, I depend upon the Holy Spirit to direct me, in and by my own experience and reflection, joined to the advices of my religious friends here and elsewhere. Only two rules it is my principle to observe in all cases: first, to begin, continue, and end all my advices in the spirit of meekness, as knowing that "the wrath" or severity "of man worketh not the righteousness of God"; and secondly, to add to meekness, long-suffering, in pursuance of a rule which I fixed long since—"never to give up anyone till I have tried him at least ten years. How long hath God had pity on thee!"

The Settled and Unsettled Tutor

Wesley's view of religion, its requirements and its restrictions, was certainly a minority position at Oxford. Consequently, he was the brunt of a great deal of criticism, even from his friends and family. Under this pressure, Wesley was continually looking for some sense of assurance, some sign that he was truly a Christian. Two traditional positions he adopted, though not fully satisfying, seemed to assuage his uneasiness: that hope of salvation rested on one's sincerity, and that persecution was a necessary mark of a Christian.

Wesley used the latter argument as part of his rationale for staying at Oxford in spite of his father's request that John succeed him as rector of Epworth. In a lengthy letter written to Samuel Wesley, Sr., whose health was weakening in his old age, John outlined in some detail the nature of his vocation and his reasons for desiring to stay at Oxford even though many despised him there. Although he saw his position in a new light six months later after his father had died, he clearly shows his sense of determination at the time in these selections from the letter.

[To Samuel Wesley, Sr., December 10, 1734]

1. The authority of a parent and the call of providence are things of so sacred a nature that a question in which these are any way concerned deserves the most serious consideration. . . .

2. I entirely agree that "the glory of God and the different degrees of promoting it are to be our sole consideration and direction in the choice of any course of life." . . .

4. That course of life tends most to the glory of God wherein we can most promote holiness in ourselves and others. . . .

6. By holiness I mean, not fasting, or bodily austerity, or any other external means of improvement, but that inward temper to which all these are subservient, a renewal of soul in the image of God. . . .

16. From all this I conclude that where I was most holy myself, there I could most promote holiness in others; and consequently that I could more promote it here than in any place under heaven. . . .

20. Notwithstanding, therefore, their present prejudice in my favour, I cannot quit my first conclusion, that I am not likely to do that good anywhere, not even at Epworth, which I may do at Oxford.

22. With regard to contempt, then . . . my first position, in defiance of worldly wisdom, is this: "Every true Christian is contemned wherever he lives by all who are not so, and who know him to be such; that is, in effect, by all with whom he converses, since it is impossible for light not to shine." . . .

23. My next position is this: "Till he be thus contemned, no man is in a state of salvation." . . .

25. And hence . . . I infer one position more, that the being despised is absolutely necessary to our doing good in the world.

26. These are a part of my reasons for choosing to abide (till I am better informed) in the station wherein God has placed me. . . .

Wesley was increasingly frustrated in his desire for self-conscious assurance that his persistently practiced methods at Oxford were in fact promoting holiness of heart and mind in his life. By the beginning of 1735, a growing concern for the "liberty" of the gospel (partly derived from the mystic writers) led him to begin testing his scheme of living; he began to question some of his practices. He began to cast lots to see if, in specific circumstances, providential determination would confirm his long-held practices of early rising or fasting. In the midst of these tensions, he disclosed both his theological quandary and his operating principles in a list of questions and answers. These he copied onto an extra page in the front of his last Oxford diary sometime during the fall or winter of 1734/35.

Q. How examine—daily, weekly, monthly?
A. Hourly only, revising in the morning.
Q. How steer between scrupulosity, as to particular instances of self-denial, and self-indulgence?
A. *Fac quod in te est, et Deus aderit bonae tuae voluntati* [Do what lieth in thy power, and God will assist thy good will].
Q. How steer between impatience and want of zeal for improvement? Between niceness in marking my progress and carelessness in it?
A. Think not at all of anything either past or future any farther than is necessary for improving the present hour.

Although his motivation for religious activity ("doing the best you can") relied heavily on "sincerity" in typical eighteenth-century fashion, the result was not, as many have claimed, simply works-righteousness. The main factor in the equation was still the grace of God. "Resume all your externals," he advised George Whitefield early in 1735, "but do not depend on them in the least." That same insight was at the heart of Wesley's comment to John Burton later that year as Wesley waited to sail for Georgia: "Nor indeed till he does all he can for God, will any man feel that he can himself do nothing."

CHAPTER 4

THE COLONIAL MISSIONARY

Wesley set sail for Georgia in the fall of 1735 with a grand vision of his role as missionary to the Indians. His parting letter to a friend, John Burton, explained that he not only had "hope of doing more" among the "heathens" in America than in England; he also hoped to "learn the true sense of the gospel of Christ" through his ministry to those unspoiled "Gentiles" and thus be able to attain a higher degree of holiness himself. Two years later, his mission was in a shambles—not only had he been yet unable to "go among the Indians," but his basic morality (not to say his holiness) was being questioned in a court of law.

Wesley's strict high-church perspective was not well received by many of the rougher settlers in the newly established colony. His single-mindedness occasionally nettled the leadership (including James Oglethorpe). His ineptness in romance resulted in a lost love, and his spiteful reaction to his loss brought a warrant for his arrest. The strange intertwining of these problems resulted in a series of grand jury indictments that led to his hasty departure from the colony.

In the midst of these trials, emotional, pastoral, and legal, Wesley wrote several different accounts describing his situation. At least five manuscript narratives have survived in addition to his daily diary. A slightly different picture emerges from each of these journals, depending upon the time it was written and the readers for whom it was intended.

The first selection below was written after only half a year in the colony and focuses on his pastoral duties. The second was compiled after a full year, just after the woman he loved had married another man. The third was drawn up five months later in the midst of his legal problems with a grand jury. The fourth selection is from an account that was written last; it became the basis for his published version. But throughout them all is the picture of a young man trying to stamp his identity upon his surroundings during a period when his own self-understanding was being severely tested.

The Hard-pressed Pastor

Before Wesley's ship had landed at Savannah, the Georgia Trustees in London had appointed him minister of the parish. Wesley probably anticipated this assignment, though he certainly hoped it would not interfere with his primary goal, to preach to the Indians. Increasingly frustrated in his attempts to go among the Indians, however, he began to turn his attention to his congregation at Savannah. He performed his ministerial functions in a zealous, if somewhat rigid, fashion. A relatively small but faithful following responded positively. From among these he even formed a small extracurricular society that met frequently in his home after the daily service of Evening Prayer. This event he later called "the second rise of Methodism" (after Oxford).

However, Wesley's method of exercising his ministerial office brought him many trials and a great deal of criticism. The following selection from his journal, drawn up in September 1736, is part of a copy that he seems to have sent as a report back to England, either to the Trustees or to friends. This narrative reflects his own understanding that he was simply doing his duty as a good Church of England priest, operating under difficult circumstances. He calls out for assistance, presumably to his friends back in England, where his brother Charles had just returned. These comments are not found in any other of the extant journal extracts that he wrote or published.

Saturday, August 21 [1736], I spent an hour with Mr. Horton and laboured to convince him I was not his enemy. But it was labour in vain; he had heard stories which he would not repeat and was consequently immovable as a rock. Many things indeed he mentioned in general, as, that I was always prying into other people's concerns in order to set them together by the ears; that I had betrayed every one who had trusted me; that I had revealed the confessions of dying men; that I had belied every one I had conversed with; himself, in particular, to whom I was determined to do all the mischief I could. But whenever I pressed him to come to particulars, he absolutely refused it. I asked him what motive he thought I had to proceed thus? He said he believed it was a pure delight in doing mischief, and added, "I believe in a morning, when you say your prayers, you resolve against it. But by the time you have been abroad two hours, all your resolutions are vanished and you can't be easy till you are at it again."

Here Mrs. Welch coming up, asked with a curse what I meant by saying she was an adulteress, and entertained me and a pretty many other auditors with such a mixture of scurrility and profaneness as I had not heard before. God deliver thee from the gall of bitterness and the bond of iniquity. . . .

On Friday [September 10, 1736] we began our Morning Prayers at quarter past five, an hour we hope to adhere to all the winter. Between fifteen and twenty persons constantly attend them, besides the children and the rest of our own family.

I had often observed that I scarce ever visited any persons, in health or sickness, but they attended Public Prayers for some time after. This increased my desire of seeing not only those who were sick, but all my parishioners as soon as possible at their own houses. Accordingly, I had long since begun to visit them in order from house to house. But I could not go on two days, the sick increasing so fast as to require all the time I have to spare (which is from one in the afternoon till five). Nor is even that enough to see them all (as I would do) daily. So that even in this town (not to mention Frederica and all the smaller settlements) there are above five hundred sheep that are (almost) without a shepherd. He that is unjust must be unjust still. Here is none to search out and lay hold on the *Mollia tempora fandi* [apt times for talk] and to persuade him to save his soul alive. He that is a babe in Christ may be so still; here is none to attend the workings of grace upon his spirit, to feed him by degrees with good convenient for him, and gently lead him till he can follow the Lamb wherever he goeth. Does any err from the right way? Here is none to recall him; he may go on to seek death in the error of his life. Is any wavering? Here is none to confirm him. Is any falling? There is none to lift him up. What a single man can do is not seen or felt. Where are ye who are very zealous for the Lord of Hosts? Who will rise up with me against the wicked? Who will take God's part against the evildoers? Whose spirit is moved within him to prepare himself for publishing glad tidings to those on whom the Sun of Righteousness never yet arose, by labouring first for those his countrymen who are else without hope as well as without God in the world? Do you ask, What you shall have? Why, all you desire. Food to eat, raiment to put on, a place where to lay your head (such as your Lord had not) and a crown of life that fadeth not away! Do you seek means of building up yourselves in the knowledge and love of God? I call the God whom we serve to witness, I know of no place under heaven where there are more, or perhaps so many, as in this place. Does your heart burn within you to turn many others to righteousness? Behold, the whole land, thousands of thousands are before you! I will resign to any of you, all or any part of my charge; choose what seemeth good in your own eyes.

The Rejected Suitor

Wesley's role as pastor in Savannah resulted in some tensions with his flock, to be sure, but it also provided the circumstances for him to cultivate a relationship with Sophia Christiana Hopkey, niece of the Chief Magistrate of the colony, Thomas Causton. They were quickly attracted to each other though she was fifteen years younger than Wesley.

Wesley's ideal of celibacy as "the more excellent way" was severely tested during the days and weeks after Wesley met Sophy. They spent many hours together in the mornings and evenings after Public Prayers. Sophy seems to have been more interested than John in a permanent relationship, although his heart was certainly not absolutely disinclined in that direction.

Through a series of misunderstandings, this amorous relationship suddenly ended in frustration and spite one year after their first meeting. Sophy married William Williamson on three days' notice—without the proper publishing of the banns, an omission that further irritated an already irate Wesley. John's subsequent discovery of Sophy's "dissimulation" (i.e., deceitful two-timing) came several weeks after she had married Williamson. In the meantime, he wrote a narrative account of their acquaintance which tended always to give her the benefit of the doubt.

This particular journal extract, like the one in section (a) above, was never published in Wesley's lifetime—it was intended only for private use and was probably sent to his close friends or perhaps his family; it sounds very much like something he would have written for his mother. The story ends with Miss Sophy's marriage in March 1737 and was written two weeks later, although the extant manuscript copy was not transcribed until one year later.

1. At my first coming to Savannah, in the beginning of March 1736, I was determined to have no intimacy with any woman in America. Notwithstanding which, by the advice of my friends and in pursuance of my resolution to speak once a week at least to every communicant apart from the congregation, on March the 13th I spoke to Miss Sophy Hopkey, who had communicated the Sunday before, and endeavoured to explain to her the nature and necessity of inward holiness. On the same subject I continued to speak to her once a week, but generally in the open air, and never alone.

2. I had a good hope that herein I acted with a single eye to the glory of God and the good of her soul. . . .

6. My friends believed it was now my duty to see her more

frequently than before; in compliance with whose advice I accordingly talked with her once in two or three days. In all those conversations I was careful to speak only on things pertaining to God. But on July ——, after I had talked with her for some time, I took her by the hand, and before we parted kissed her. And from this time, I fear there was a mixture in my intention, though I was not soon sensible of it. . . .

13. After giving her in writing, as she desired, a few advices relating to the presence of God, I left Frederica, September 2, not doubting but he who had begun a good work in her would establish her heart unblamable in holiness unto the day of the Lord Jesus. I then found I had not only a high esteem but a tender affection for her; but it was as for a sister and this I thought strictly due both to her piety and her friendship. . . .

18. In the evening we landed on an uninhabited island, made a fire, supped, went to Prayers together, and then spread our sail over us on four stakes to keep off the night dews. . . .

19. I can never be sensible enough of the exceeding goodness of God, both this night and the four following, all which we spent together, while none but the All-Seeing Eye observed us. I know that in me there was no strength; God knoweth if there were more in her. To him alone be the praise, that we were both withheld from anything which the world counts evil. Yet am I not thereby justified, but must justify God for whatever temporal evils may befall me on her account. . . .

27. Monday, November 1, she was eighteen years old. And from the beginning of our intimate acquaintance till this day, I verily believe she used no guile. [At this point, Wesley fills five pages describing Sophy, the portrait perhaps revealing Wesley's idea of the virtuous person as much as (or more than) Sophy's actual qualities.] . . . She was all life: active, diligent, indefatigable . . . ; nor did she at all favour herself . . . ; she was patient of labour, of cold, heat, wet, of badness or want of food, and of pain to an eminent degree . . . ; though always neat, she was always plain . . . ; she had a large share of common sense, and particularly of prudence; . . . she was so teachable in things either of a practical or speculative nature, so readily convinced of any error in her judgment or oversight in her behaviour . . . ; as her humility was, so was her meekness; she seemed to have been born

without anger . . . ; she was a friend to humankind; to whoever was distressed, she was all sympathy, tenderness, compassion . . . ; the utmost anguish never wrung from her a murmuring word; she saw the hand of God and was still. . . .

34. Such was the woman, according to my closest observation, of whom I now began to be much afraid. My desire and design still was to live single. But how long it would continue, I knew not. I therefore consulted my friends whether it was not best to break off all intercourse with her immediately. Three months after, they told me, "It would have been best." But at this time they expressed themselves so ambiguously that I understood them to mean the direct contrary, viz., that I ought not to break it off. And accordingly she came to me (as had been agreed) every morning and evening. . . .

36. This I began with a single eye. But it was not long before I found it a task too hard for me, to preserve the same intention with which I began, in such intimacy of conversation as ours was. My greatest difficulty was, . . . when being obliged (as having but one book) to sit close to her, unless I prayed without ceasing, I could not avoid using some familiarity or other which was not needful. Sometimes I put my arm round her waist, sometimes took her by the hand, and sometimes kissed her. To put a short stop to this, on November 10, I . . . told her, . . . "Some parts of my behaviour might make you question my sincerity. Those I dislike, and have therefore resolved never to touch you more." She appeared surprised and deeply serious, but said not one word.

37. . . . When [Phoebe Hird] asked her, "What if Mr. Wesley would have her," she smiled, looked down, and said nothing. I told Mr. Delamotte when we were alone that now I perceived myself to be in real danger since it was probable, even from that little circumstance, that the marriage stopped, not at her, but at me. . . .

46. I was now more clear in my judgment every day. Beside that I believed her resolved never to marry, I was convinced it was not expedient for me. . . . And on Monday [February] 14, about seven in the morning, I told her in my own garden, I am resolved, Miss Sophy, if I marry at all, not to do it till I have been among the Indians. . . .

51. Saturday, [February] 26. Calling at Mr. Causton's, she was

then alone. And this was indeed an hour of trial. Her words, her eyes, her air, her every motion and gesture, were full of such a softness and sweetness! I know not what might have been the consequence, had I then but touched her hand. And how I avoided it, I know not. Surely God is over all!

52. . . . I was so utterly disarmed, that this hour I should have engaged myself for life, had it not been for the full persuasion I had of her entire sincerity, in consequence of which I doubted not but she was resolved (as she had said) "Never to marry while she lived."

53. . . . I told [Mr. Delamotte] I had no intention to marry her. He said I did not know my own heart; but he saw clearly it would come to that very soon unless I broke off all intercourse with her. I told him this was a point of great importance and therefore not to be determined suddenly. He said I ought to determine as soon as possible, for I was losing ground daily. I felt what he said to be true and therefore easily consented to set aside the next day for that purpose. . . . At length we agreed to appeal to the Searcher of Hearts. I accordingly made three lots. In one was writ, "Marry"; in the second, "Think not of it this year." After we had prayed to God to "give us a perfect lot," Mr. Delamotte drew the third, in which were these words: "Think of it no more." Instead of the agony I had reason to expect, I was enabled to say cheerfully, "Thy will be done."

55. On Monday the 7th [of March, Miss Sophy said,] "Well, I find what you have often said is true. There is no trusting any but a Christian. And for my part I am resolved never to trust anyone again who is not so." I looked upon her, and should have said too much had we had a moment longer. But in the instant, Mrs. Causton called us in. So I was once more "snatched as a brand out of the fire."

56. Tuesday, March 8. Miss Sophy breakfasting with me, . . . I said, "I hear Mr. Williamson pays his addresses to you. Is it true?" She said, after a little pause, "If it were not, I would have told you so. . . . I have no inclination for him." I said, "Miss Sophy, if you deceive me, I shall scarce ever believe anyone again." She looked up at me and answered with a smile, "You will never have that reason for distrusting anyone. I shall never deceive you." When she was going away, she turned back and said, "Of one thing, sir,

be assured, I will never take any step in anything of importance without first consulting you."

59. The next morning, Wednesday, March 9, about ten, I called on Mrs. Causton. She said, "[Sophy] desires you would publish the banns of marriage between her and Mr. Williamson Sunday. . . . But if you have any objection to it, pray speak. Speak to her . . . ; she will be very glad to hear anything Mr. Wesley has to say. . . ."

60. I doubted whether all this were not artifice, merely designed to quicken me. But though I was uneasy at the very thought of her marrying one who I believed would make her very unhappy, yet I could not resolve to save her from him by marrying her myself. Besides, I reasoned thus, "Either she is engaged or not. If she is, I would not have her if I might; if not, there is nothing in this show which ought to alter my preceding resolution."

61. Thus was I saved purely by my ignorance; for though I did doubt, I would not believe. . . .

68. . . . The next morning she set out for Purrysburg, and on Saturday, March 12, 1737, was married there, this being the day which completed the year from my first speaking to her!

[Wesley's diary entry for Wednesday, March 9, 1737, the day he discovered Miss Sophy was to marry Mr. Williamson:]
4 Private prayer; prayers; diary. 4.45 Private prayer. 5 Meditated; Public Prayers. 6 Coffee, religious talk. 6.30 Clement. 7 Necessary talk (religious) with Mrs. Andrews. 7.45 With Mrs. Bush, necessary talk (religious). 8.30 Clement. 9.45 Logic. 10 Mrs. Causton's, necessary talk with her; Miss Sophy to be married! 11 Amazed, in pain, prayed, meditated. 12 At the lot, necessary talk (religious) with her; I quite distressed! 1 Necessary talk (religious); confounded! 2 Took leave of her. 2.30 At home, could not pray! 3 Tried to pray, lost, sunk! 4 Bread; religious talk with Delamotte; little better. 5 Mr. Causton came, necessary talk, tea. 6 Kempis; Germans; easier! 7 Public Prayers. 8 Miss Sophy, etc. 8.30 Necessary talk (religious) with her. 8.45 With Delamotte, prayers.

> No such day since I first saw the sun!
> O deal tenderly with thy servant!
> Let me not see such another!

The Wrongfully Accused Defendant

When Wesley discovered in April that Sophy had in fact been "two-timing" him for some weeks before her "sudden" turnabout marriage, he exercised his prerogative as parish priest. He warned her that such sinful behavior as she had exhibited (including also her frequent absence from Holy Communion) would force him to exclude her from the Sacrament unless she confessed her sin. His action was a proper, though blatantly spiteful application of the directions in the Prayer Book. The inevitable confrontation at the altar occurred. Wesley publicly repelled Miss Sophy from the Table, and thereby unleashed a floodtide of events that quite literally swept him out of the colony and back to England before the legal implications of many of his controversial actions as a pastor/priest/suitor could be fully resolved in the colonial court.

Sophy's husband, Mr. Williamson, brought charges against Wesley to a grand jury that returned ten "true bills of indictment" against Wesley. As the jury deliberations were taking place in August 1737, Wesley drew up a legal brief to use as a part of his defense in the expected trial. The manuscript of his "Case," as he called it in his diary, sketches in detail the development of his relationship with Miss Sophy, drawn in such a fashion as to portray his actions and intentions as the completely innocent acts of a diligent priest, good pastor, and trusting friend.

The outline of his defense was (1) that he, Wesley, had had no designs on Miss Sophy other than to preserve her soul from various influences in the colony and to protect her happiness in whatever ways he could; (2) that Sophy had been deceitful and misleading in many of her words and actions toward Wesley; and (3) that Mr. Causton (who was Sophy's legal guardian and who also presided over the grand jury) was not only a silent party with the prosecution, but in fact had been, with his wife, the primary instigator of false charges against Wesley and, through his "artful disingenuity," had been just as deceitful as his niece in the whole affair, since Causton had allowed his household to become a sounding board for many of the charges trumped up against Wesley.

From the opening sentence, Wesley's "Case," intended to be read in the courtroom, constructs the picture of a long-suffering, ill-used servant of God (and friend of the Trustees) who has been misled by the wiles of a beautiful young woman, confused by the matchmaking of her two-faced aunt, and wrongfully treated by the maliciousness of the political powers in the colony. Wesley claimed the proceedings against him were illegal since most of the charges were of an ecclesiastical nature and should not be tried in a civil court (see the list of indictments on page 122, below). Wesley also wanted to make it clear, on record in the courtroom, that it was Mr. Causton's distrust of the Trustees' supposedly "dilatory manner" that made the magistrate unwilling to submit the case to the proper authorities.

1. It was not my desire, but the desire of the Trustees, disappointed of another minister, which induced me to take charge of Savannah, till I could pursue my first design. And [the] very day I entered on this charge I told you that offences would come; indeed I expected greater, long before this day.

2. In March 1736, observing Miss Sophy Hopkey to be a constant communicant, I thought it my duty to speak to her apart from the congregation; I did so from that time once a week. . . .

3. . . . In June following, [Mrs. Causton] told me, "Sir, you want a woman to take care of your house." I said, "But women, madam, are scarce in Georgia. Where shall I get one?" She answered, "I have two here. Take either of them. . . . Take Phily [Sophy], she is serious enough." I said, "You are not in earnest, madam!" She said, "Indeed, sir, I am; take her to you and do what you will with her."

5. Friday, August 13. I came to Frederica, where Mr. Oglethorpe gave me a large account of Miss Sophy and desired me to be with her as much as I could, "Because she was in deep distress."

6. The time I was with her was spent chiefly in reading. The books I now read and explained to her were first, *A Collection of*

Prayers, next *Tracts on the Presence of God,* and then Dr. Cave's *Primitive Christianity.*

9. Tuesday, October 12, about five in the evening, being to set out for Frederica the next day, I asked Mr. Causton what commands he had to Miss Sophy? Some of his words were as follows: "The girl will never be easy till she is married." . . . I asked, "Sir, what directions do you give me with regard to her?" He said, "I give her up to you. Do what you will with her. Take her into your own hands. Promise her what you will; I will make it good."

18. The time she spent at my house was spent thus: immediately after breakfast we all joined in prayer. She was then alone till eight. I taught her French between eight and nine, and at nine we joined in prayer again. She then either read or wrote French till ten. In the evening I read to her and some others, several parts of Ephrem Syrus, and afterwards Dean Young's and Mr. Reeves' Sermons. We always concluded our reading with a psalm. . . .

20. . . . On Thursday, February 3, . . . I hinted at a desire to marry her, but made no direct proposal. For indeed it was only a sudden thought which had not the consent of my own mind. Yet I verily believe had she closed with me at that time, my judgment would have been overruled. But she said she thought it was best for clergymen not to be incumbered with worldly cares; and that it was best for her too, and she was resolved never to marry while she lived. I made no reply, nor used any argument to induce her to alter her resolution. . . .

22. If it be asked, why I did not propose it, though I had so great a regard for her, I answer, for three reasons chiefly: (1) Because I did not think myself strong enough to bear the temptations of a married state; (2) because I feared it would have obstructed the design on which I came, the going among the Indians; and (3) because I thought her resolved not to marry. . . .

30. [On March 9, 1737,] about ten, I called on Mrs. Causton. She said, "Sir, Mr. Causton and I are exceedingly obliged to you for all the pains you have taken about Sophy. And so is Sophy too; and she desires you would publish the banns of marriage between her and Mr. Williamson on Sunday." She added, "Sir, you don't seem well-pleased. Have you any objections to it?" I answered, "Madam, I don't seem to be awake. Surely I am in a dream." She

said, "They agreed on it between themselves last night, and later Mr. Williamson asked Mr. Causton's and my consent, which we gave him. But if you have any objection to it, pray speak. Speak to her. She is at the lot. Go to her. She will be very glad to hear anything Mr. Wesley has to say. . . ."

31. If I may speak what was then the inmost thought of my heart, it was that all this was mere artifice, purely designed to quicken me; and that as much engaged as she was, had I only said, "I am willing to marry her myself," that engagement would have vanished away. But though I was very uneasy at the very mention of her marrying Mr. Williamson, who I believed would make her thoroughly miserable, yet I could not resolve to save her from him by marrying her myself. This was the only price I could not pay, and which therefore I never so much as hinted at in any of those following conversations wherein I so earnestly endeavoured to prevent that unhappy union. . . .

[On July 5] I sent the following note to Mrs. Williamson, which I wrote in the most mild and friendly manner I could, both in pursuance of my resolution to proceed with all mildness, and because Mrs. Causton told me she was so much grieved already.

"If the sincerity of friendship is best to be known from the painful offices, then there could not be a stronger proof of mine than that I gave you on Sunday, except this which I am going to give you now and which you may perhaps equally misinterpret. . . .

"In your present behaviour I dislike, (1) your neglect of half the Public Service . . . (2) your neglect of fasting . . . (3) your neglect of almost half the opportunities of communicating which you have lately had.

"But these things are small in comparison of what I dislike in your past behaviour. For (1) you told me over and over you had entirely conquered your inclination for Mr. Mellichamp. Yet at the very time you spoke, you had not conquered it. (2) You told me frequently you had no design to marry Mr. Williamson. Yet at the very time you spoke, you had that design. (3) In order to conceal both these things from me, you went though a course of deliberate dissimulation. O how fallen! How changed! Surely there was a time when in Miss Sophy's lips there was no guile. . . ."

58. On Sunday evening [August 7], Mrs. Williamson, in conversation with Mrs. Burnside, expressed much anger at my repelling her from the Holy Communion. Mrs. Burnside told her, "You was much to blame after receiving that letter from Mr. Wesley, to offer yourself at the Table before you had cleared yourself to him. But you may easily put an end to this by going to Mr. Wesley now and clearing yourself of what you are charged with." She replied, "No, I will not show such a meanness of spirit as to speak to him about it myself, but somebody else shall."

59. The next day, August 8, the following warrant was issued out by Mr. Recorder:

"To all constables, tithingmen, and others whom these may concern:

"You, and each of you, are hereby required, to take the body of John Westly, Clerk, and bring him before one of the bailiffs of the said town to answer the complaint of William Williamson and Sophia his wife, for defaming the said Sophia and refusing to administer to her the Sacrament of the Lord's Supper in a public congregation without cause; by which the said William Williamson is damaged one thousand pounds sterling. . . ."

65. I was now the constant subject of conversation at Mr. Causton's, where the account given of me to all company was, that I "was a sly hypocrite, a seducer, a betrayer of my trust, an egregious liar and dissembler, an endeavourer to alienate the affections of married women from their husbands, a drunkard, the keeper of a bawdy-house, an admitter of whores, whore-mongers, drunkards, ay and of murderers and spillers of blood to the Lord's Table, a repeller of others out of mere spite and malice, a refuser of Christian burial to Christians, a murderer of poor infants by plunging them into cold water, a Papist, if not a Jesuit, or rather, an introducer of a new religion which as nobody ever heard of, a proud priest whose view it was to be a bishop, a spiritual tyrant, an arbitrary usurper of illegal power, a false teacher enjoining others under peril of damnation to do what I would omit myself to serve a turn, a denier of the king's supremacy, an enemy to the colony, a sower of sedition, a public incendiary, a disturber of the peace of families, a raiser of uproars, a ringleader of mutiny"; in a word, such a monster, "that the people would rather die than suffer him to go on thus."

66. Coming home in the evening, I found Mr. Causton with Mr. Parker and Mr. Jones at my house. He broke out, "Wesley, I am ashamed of this. I could not have believed it of thee. Why is all this uproar? . . . I have been insulted in the streets; I have been called Judas to my face. And why must one of my family be the first to be repelled from the Holy Communion?" He added many reproaches and upbraidings. The sum of my answer was, "I am sorry if there has been any disturbance and will do all that in me lies to preserve peace and the respect due to all Magistrates, whom I reverence as the ministers of God."

68. After he went, I writ the following note, the second and last proposal of accommodation I have made:

"To Mrs. Sophia Williamson: At Mr. Causton's request I write once more. The rules whereby I proceed are these: 'So many as intend to be partakers of the Holy Communion shall signify their names to the curate at least some time the day before.' This you did not do. . . .

"If you offer yourself at the Lord's Table on Sunday, I will advertise you (as I have done more than once) wherein you 'have done wrong'; and when you have 'openly declared yourself to have truly repented,' I will administer to you the mysteries of God. . . ."

Mrs. Williamson insisted she had done nothing amiss. Mr. Causton said, "I am the person that am injured, I am ill used; the affront is offered to me, and I will espouse the cause of my niece. It will be the worse thing Mr. Wesley ever did in his life, to fix upon my family. . . . I am injured, and I will have satisfaction, if it is to be had in the world." "And I," said Mr. Williamson, "will never leave him to my life's end."

The Ostracized Reporter

Wesley explains his hasty retreat from Georgia in another pair of manuscript journals that are less selective in content. This version of his story provided the basis for the published "extract" of his Georgia journal in 1740 (see below, page 117). The published version differs somewhat from both the manuscripts. The portion in brackets was omitted from the published version. The portion in parentheses is in the published version but not in the manuscripts.

Friday, October 7. I consulted my friends whether God did not call me to (return to) England [not on my own account, but for the sake of the poor people]. (The reason for which I left it had now no force, there being no possibility, as yet, of instructing the Indians; neither had I, as yet, found or heard of any Indians on the continent of America who had the least desire of being instructed. And as to Savannah, having never engaged myself, either by word or letter, to stay there a day longer than I should judge convenient, nor ever taken charge of the people any otherwise than as in my passage to the heathen, I looked upon myself to be fully discharged therefrom by the vacating of that design. Besides, there was a probability of doing more service to that unhappy people in England than I could do in Georgia, by representing, without fear or favour to the Trustees, the real state the colony was in. . . . I laid the thoughts of it aside for the present, being persuaded that when the time was come, God would 'make the way plain before my face'. . . .)

Tuesday, November 22. (. . . I again consulted my friends, who agreed with me that the time we looked for was now come. . . .)

Friday, December 2. I proposed to set out for [Port Royal] (Carolina) about noon, the tide then serving. But about ten the magistrates sent for me and told me I must not go out of the province [till I had entered into recognizance to appear at the Court] for I had not answered the allegations laid against me. I replied, "I have appeared at [four] (six or seven) Courts successively in order to answer them. But I was not suffered so to do, when I desired it time after time." [But as they had now referred them to the Trustees, to the Trustees I desired to go.] Then they said, however, I must not go, unless I would give security to answer those allegations at their Court. . . . I then told them plainly, "Sir [all this is mere trifling], you use me very ill, and so you do the Trustees. I will give neither any bond nor any bail at all. You know your business, and I know mine."

In the afternoon the magistrates published an order requiring all the officers and sentinels to prevent my going out of the province, and forbidding any person to assist me so to do. Being now only a prisoner at large in a place where I knew by experience every day would give fresh opportunity to procure evidence of words I never said and actions I never did, I saw clearly the hour was come for [me to fly for my life,] leaving this place; and as soon as evening prayers were over, about eight o'clock, the tide then serving, I shook off the dust of my feet and left Georgia, after having preached the gospel there [with much weakness indeed and many infirmities] (not as I ought, but as I was able), one year and nearly nine months.

CHAPTER 5

THEOLOGICAL AND SPIRITUAL PILGRIM

The year 1738 was another crucial period in Wesley's life. He began the year in the mid-Atlantic, on board the ship *Samuel* returning from his frustrating mission to Georgia. During the subsequent spring and summer, he came to know and feel the "assurance of faith" in its "true" sense (according to his Moravian friends). During the autumn he became acquainted with the work of the Holy Spirit in the Great Awakening in New England through the writings of Jonathan Edwards. Shortly thereafter, he rediscovered in the Homilies of the Church of England an understanding of faith and salvation nearly identical to what he had been putting together for himself for the past decade or more.

Three times during this period Wesley paused to analyze his spiritual condition and evaluate his spiritual progress. In early June he wrote an account of his "Aldersgate experience," familiar to many readers of Wesley's *Journal*. It represents his outlook almost immediately after his "heart was strangely warmed." Just five months earlier in the mid-Atlantic, he had written an autobiographical summary that similarly reviewed his spiritual progress. After the year was over, he again reflected on his spiritual condition in a summary later published in his *Journal*. The reflections in these three accounts help us measure and put in perspective the significance of the events of this important year in Wesley's continuing spiritual and theological development.

One Tossed About; Theological Autobiography, January 1738

Wesley's experience in Georgia tested his self-understanding in several ways, not least of which was theological. His contacts with the German Pietists among the colonists (Moravians and Salzburgers) had made him very much aware that his own religious faith was inadequate in times of stress. At this point in his life, he still tended to treat the question of salvation as primarily an intellectual, theological problem. His Oxford years had instilled in him the value of tracing through a problem logically, in written form. Thus, as Wesley's ship approached the shores of England on his return from Georgia, he penned what amounts to a scholastic exercise, a *genesis problematica,* summarizing his plight in a survey of his doctrinal development up to that time.

Wesley's main question was that of the rich young ruler, "What must I do to be saved?" At this time, Wesley saw the problem as twofold: what is the proper understanding and relationship of faith and works, and upon what authority should a correct theological answer be based? He was still working on the assumption that his *assurance* of salvation (*knowing* he was a Christian) was a sort of intellectual confidence that depended upon holding a correct set of beliefs, grounded upon the appropriately ranked authorities (scripture, tradition, reason) and resulting in a proper set of actions. His *hope* for salvation was still placed in a *trust* that his own *sincerity* would suffice, that he was in fact "doing the best he could," as Kempis had instructed in the *Imitatio Christi* ("*Fac quod in te est,*" I.vii.2). He had only recently been introduced to the idea that faith and hope might rest on a more personal appropriation of the atoning work of Christ, experienced through the Holy Spirit. But there is not yet even a hint of that perspective in this shipboard survey of his condition.

Μὴ κλυδωνιζόμενοι παντὶ ἀνέμῳ τῆς διδαχῆς.
["Not tossed to and fro by every wind of doctrine"; cf. Eph. 4:14]

Different views of Christianity are given (1) by the Scripture, (2) the Papists, (3) the Lutherans and Calvinists, (4) the English Divines, (5) the Essentialist-Nonjurors, (6) the Mystics.

January 25, 1738

1. For many years have I been tossed about by various winds of doctrine. I asked long ago, What must I do to be saved? The Scripture answered, "Keep the Commandments. Believe, hope, love. Follow after these tempers till thou hast fully attained, that is, till death, by all those outward works and means which God hath appointed, by walking as Christ walked."

2. I was early warned against laying, as the Papists do, too much stress either on outward works or on a faith without works, which, as it does not include, so it will never lead to, true hope or charity. Nor am I sensible that to this hour I have laid too much stress on either, having from the very beginning valued both faith, the means of grace, and good works, not on their own account, but as believing God, who had appointed them, would by them bring me in due time to the mind that was in Christ.

3. But before God's time was come, I fell among some Lutheran and Calvinist authors, whose confused and indigested accounts magnified faith to such an amazing size that it quite hid all the rest of the commandments. I did not then see that this was the natural effect of their overgrown fear of [or zeal against] Popery; being so tempted with the cry of "merit and good works" that they plunged at once into the other extreme. In this labyrinth I was utterly lost: not being able to find out what the error was, not yet to reconcile this uncouth hypothesis either with Scripture or common sense.

4. The English writers, such as Bishop Beveridge, Bishop Taylor, and Mr. Nelson, a little relieved me from these well-meaning, wrong-headed Germans. Their accounts of Christianity I could easily see to be, in the main, consistent both with reason and Scripture. Only, when they interpreted Scripture in different ways, I was often much at a loss. And again, there was

one thing much insisted on in Scripture, the unity of the Church, which none of them I thought clearly explained or strongly inculcated.

5. But it was not long before Providence brought me to those who showed me a sure rule for interpreting Scripture, viz. *Consensus veterum: "Quod ab omnibus, quod ubique, quod semper creditum"* [The consensus of antiquity: "What is believed by everyone, everywhere, and always"]. At the same time they sufficiently insisted upon a due regard to the one Church at all times and in all places. Nor was it long before I bent the bow too far the other way (1) by making antiquity a co-ordinate (rather than subordinate) rule with Scripture, (2) by admitting several doubtful writings as undoubted evidences of antiquity, (3) by extending antiquity too far, even to the middle or end of the fourth century, (4) by believing more practices to have been universal in the ancient Church than ever were so, (5) by not considering that the decrees of one provincial synod could bind only that province, and the decrees of a general synod only those provinces whose representatives met therein, (6) by not considering that most of those decrees were adapted to particular times and occasions, and consequently when those occasions ceased, must cease to bind even those provinces.

6. These considerations insensibly stole upon me as I grew acquainted with the mystic writers, whose noble descriptions of union with God and internal religion made everything else appear mean, flat, and insipid. But in truth, they made good works appear so too, yea, and faith itself, and what not? These gave me an entire new view of religion, nothing like any I had had before. But alas! It was nothing like that religion which Christ and his Apostles lived and taught. I had a plenary dispensation from all the commands of God. The form ran thus, "Love is all; all the commands beside are only means of love. You must choose those which you feel are means to you and use them as long as they are so." Thus were all the bands burst at once. And though I could never fully come into this, nor contentedly omit what God enjoined, yet I know not how, I fluctuated between obedience and disobedience. I had no heart, no vigour, no zeal in obeying; continually doubting, whether I was right or wrong, and never out of perplexities and entanglements. Nor can I at this hour give a distinct account, how

or when I came a little back toward the right way. Only, my present sense is this, All the other enemies of Christianity are triflers; the mystics are the most dangerous of all its enemies. They stab it in the vitals and its most serious professors are most likely to fall by them. May I praise Him who hath snatched me out of this fire likewise, by warning all others, that it is set on fire of hell.

The Assured Conqueror;
Spiritual Autobiography, May 1738

Wesley's desire to experience "assurance" of his salvation was fulfilled in May 1738, three days after his brother Charles had felt "a strange palpitation of heart" on Pentecost Sunday (see volume 2, page 63). Within just a few days, John wrote an account of these events, recounting in eighteen numbered paragraphs the important steps in his life that had led up to this experience, and describing his "new" state of self-knowledge. He read this narrative to his mother when he visited her in early June (see below, page 113). Wesley was able now to conceive of himself as having truly met the criteria necessary for calling oneself a "Christian," as defined by his Moravian friends. He began to proclaim their doctrine as his own, namely that one is not a Christian until he or she has experienced assurance, a doctrine that marked his preaching for several years to come, but that he later altered.

That Wesley felt this experience was pivotal in his spiritual development at this time is obvious in the document itself. That he continued to think so, in some qualified sense, for at least some months is also evident from his own writings (see his letter to brother Samuel, April 4, 1739). That he eventually abandoned his hard line on the necessity of assurance as a prerequisite for salvation comes through very clearly in the minutes of conference as early as 1744 and in letters to his brother Charles (e.g., July 31, 1747). That he later began to qualify some of his own self-analysis from this earlier period is very clear from subsequent alterations he made in the published text of the *Journal* itself (viz., the *errata* sheet in

1775). That his seasoned view could see the whole train of events with a sense of humorous self-criticism is evident in a comment to a friend, Melville Horne, in his old age: "When fifty years ago my brother Charles and I, in [the] simplicity of our hearts, told the good people of England that unless they *knew* their sins were forgiven they were under the wrath and curse of God, I marvel, Melville, they did not stone us!" (Southey, I, 295).

What occurred on Wednesday the 24th [of May 1738], I think best to relate at large, after premising what may make it the better understood. Let him that cannot receive it ask of the Father of lights that He would give more light to him and me.

1. I believe, till I was about ten years old I had not sinned away that "washing of the Holy Ghost" which was given me in baptism; having been strictly educated and carefully taught that I could only be saved "by universal obedience, by keeping all the commandments of God"; in the meaning of which I was diligently instructed. And those instructions, so far as they respected outward duties and sins, I gladly received and often thought of. But all that was said to me of inward obedience or holiness I neither understood nor remembered. So that I was indeed as ignorant of the true meaning of the law as I was of the gospel of Christ.

2. The next six or seven years were spent at school, where, outward restraints being removed, I was much more negligent than before, even of outward duties, and almost continually guilty of outward sins, which I knew to be such, though they were not scandalous in the eye of the world. However, I still read the Scriptures, and said my prayers morning and evening. And what I now hoped to be saved by, was (1) not being so bad as other people; (2) having still a kindness for religion; and (3) reading the Bible, going to church, and saying my prayers.

3. Being removed to the University for five years, I still said my prayers both in public and in private, and read, with the Scriptures, several other books of religion, especially comments on the New Testament. Yet I had not all this while so much as a notion of inward holiness; nay, went on habitually, and for the most part very contentedly, in some or other known sin. . . . I

cannot well tell what I hoped to be saved by now, when I was continually sinning against the little light I had; unless by those transient fits of what many divines taught me to call repentance.

4. When I was about twenty-two, my father pressed me to enter into holy orders. At the same time, the providence of God directing me to Kempis' *Christian Pattern,* I began to see that true religion was seated in the heart, and that God's law extended to all our thoughts as well as words and actions. . . . I began to alter the whole form of my conversation and to set in earnest upon a new life. . . . I began to aim at and pray for inward holiness. So that now, "doing so much, and living so good a life," I doubted not but I was a good Christian.

5. Removing soon after to another College, I executed a resolution which I was before convinced was of the utmost importance—shaking off at once all my trifling acquaintance. I began to see more and more the value of time. I applied myself closer to study. I watched more carefully against actual sins; I advised others to be religious, according to that scheme of religion by which I modelled my own life. But meeting now with Mr. Law's *Christian Perfection* and *Serious Call,* although I was much offended at many parts of both, yet they convinced me more than ever of the exceeding height and breadth and depth of the law of God. The light flowed in so mightily upon my soul, that everything appeared in a new view. I cried to God for help, and resolved not to prolong the time of obeying Him as I had never done before. And by my continued endeavour to keep His whole law, inward and outward, to the utmost of my power, I was persuaded that I should be accepted of Him, and that I was even then in a state of salvation.

6. In 1730 I began visiting the prisons, assisting the poor and sick in town, and doing what other good I could by my presence or my little fortune to the bodies and souls of all men. To this end I abridged myself of all superfluities, and many that are called necessaries of life. I soon became a by-word for so doing. . . . I diligently strove against all sin. . . . I carefully used, both in public and in private, all the means of grace at all opportunities. I omitted no occasion of doing good. . . . Yet when, after continuing some years in this course, I apprehended myself to be near death, I could not find that all this gave me any comfort or any assurance of acceptance with God. . . .

7. Soon after, a contemplative man convinced me still more than I was convinced before, that outward works are nothing, being alone; and in several conversations instructed me how to pursue inward holiness, or a union of the soul with God. But even of his instructions (though I then received them as the words of God) I cannot but now observe . . . these were, in truth, as much my own works as visiting the sick or clothing the naked; and the union with God thus pursued was as really my own righteousness as any I had before pursued under another name.

8. In this refined way of trusting to my own works and my own righteousness (so zealously inculcated by the Mystic writers) I dragged on heavily, finding no comfort or help therein till the time of my leaving England. On shipboard, however, I was again active in outward works; where it pleased God of His free mercy to give me twenty-six of the Moravian brethren for companions, who endeavoured to show me "a more excellent way." But I understood it not at first. I was too learned and too wise. . . .

9. All the time I was at Savannah I was thus beating the air. Being ignorant of the righteousness of Christ, which, by a living faith in Him, bringeth salvation "to every one that believeth," I sought to establish my own righteousness; and so laboured in the fire all my days. I was now properly "under the law." . . .

10. In this vile, abject state of bondage to sin, I was indeed fighting continually, but not conquering. . . . During this whole struggle between nature and grace, which had now continued above ten years, I had many remarkable returns to prayer, especially when I was in trouble; I had many sensible comforts, which are indeed no other than short anticipations of the life of faith. But I was still "under the law," not "under grace" (the state most who are called Christians are content to live and die in): for I was only striving with, not freed from, sin. Neither had I the witness of the Spirit with my spirit, and indeed could not; for I "sought it not by faith, but as it were by the works of the law."

11. In my return to England, January 1738, being in imminent danger of death, and very uneasy on that account, I was strongly convinced that the cause of that uneasiness was unbelief, and that the gaining a true, living faith was the "one thing needful" for me. But still I fixed not this faith on its right object: I meant only faith in God, not faith in or through Christ. Again, I knew not that I was

wholly void of this faith; but only thought I had not enough of it. So that when Peter Böhler, whom God prepared for me as soon as I came to London, affirmed of true faith in Christ (which is but one) that it had those two fruits inseparably attending it, "dominion over sin and constant peace from a sense of forgiveness," I was quite amazed and looked upon it as a new gospel. If this was so, it was clear I had not faith. But I was not willing to be convinced of this. Therefore I disputed with all my might, and laboured to prove that faith might be where these were not; . . . I well saw no one could, in the nature of things, have such a sense of forgiveness, and not feel it. But I felt it not. If, then, there was no faith without this, all my pretensions to faith dropped at once.

12. When I met Peter Böhler again, he consented to put the dispute upon the issue which I desired, namely, Scripture and experience. I first consulted the Scripture. But when I set aside the glosses of men and simply considered the words of God, comparing them together, endeavouring to illustrate the obscure by the plainer passages, I found they all made against me, and was forced to retreat to my last hold, "that experience would never agree with the *literal interpretation* of those Scriptures. Nor could I therefore allow it to be true till I found some living witnesses of it." He replied he could show me such at any time; if I desired it, the next day. And accordingly the next day he came again with three others, all of whom testified of their own personal experience that a true living faith in Christ is inseparable from a sense of pardon for all past and freedom from all present sins. They added with one mouth that this faith was the gift, the free gift of God; and that He would surely bestow it upon every soul who earnestly and perseveringly sought it. I was now thoroughly convinced, and by the grace of God, I resolved to seek it unto the end (1) by absolutely renouncing all dependence in whole or in part upon *my own* works or righteousness; on which I had really grounded my hope of salvation, though I knew it not, from my youth up; (2) by adding to the constant use of all the other means of grace, continual prayer for this very thing, justifying, saving faith, a full reliance on the blood of Christ shed for *me*; a trust in Him as *my* Christ, as *my* sole justification, sanctification, and redemption.

13. I continued thus to seek it (though with strange indifference, dullness, and coldness, and unusually frequent relapses into

sin) till Wednesday, May 24. I think it was about five this morning, that I opened my Testament on those words, Τὰ μέγδτα ἡμίν καὶ τίμια ἐπαγγέλματα δεδώρηται, ἵνα γένηδθε θείας κοινωνοὶ φύδεως, "There are given unto us exceeding great and precious promises, even that ye should be partakers of the divine nature" (II Peter 1:4). Just as I went out, I opened it again on those words, "Thou are not far from the kingdom of God." In the afternoon I was asked to go to St. Paul's. The anthem was, "Out of the deep have I called unto Thee, O Lord; Lord, hear my voice. . . ."

14. In the evening I went very unwillingly to a society in Aldersgate Street, where one was reading Luther's preface to the *Epistle to the Romans.* About a quarter before nine, while he was describing the change which God works in the heart through faith in Christ, I felt my heart strangely warmed. I felt I did trust in Christ, Christ alone for salvation; and an assurance was given me that He had taken away *my* sins, even *mine,* and saved *me* from the law of sin and death.

15. I began to pray with all my might for those who had in a more especial manner despitefully used me and persecuted me. I then testified openly to all there what I now first felt in my heart. But it was not long before the enemy suggested, "This cannot be faith; for where is thy joy?" Then was I taught that peace and victory over sin are essential to faith in the Captain of our salvation, but that, as to the transports of joy that usually attend the beginning of it, especially in those who have mourned deeply, God sometimes giveth, sometimes withholdeth them, according to the counsels of His own will.

16. After my return home, I was much buffeted with temptations; but cried out, and they fled away. They returned again and again. I as often lifted up my eyes, and He "sent me help from His holy place." And herein I found the difference between this and my former state chiefly consisted. I was striving, yea, fighting with all my might under the law as well as under grace. But then I was sometimes, if not often, conquered; now, I was always conqueror.

The Humbled Doubter

Many were surprised at the claims that John began making after his "heart-warming" experience of assurance. Wesley's friend, Mrs. Hutton, wrote to his brother Samuel that very weekend saying that John "seems to be turned a wild enthusiast or fanatic, [telling] the people that five days before he was not a Christian." To this she had responded, "If you was not a Christian ever since I knew you, you was a great hypocrite, for you made us all believe you was one" (see volume 2, pages 66-67).

The *Journal* tells the continuing story of John's quest for lasting peace and joy in his newfound state, a story punctuated by frequently recurring moments of despair: "I waked in peace, but not in joy"; "I felt a kind of soreness in my heart, so that I found my wound was not fully healed" (see also below, page 198).

As the year 1739 began, John noted in his diary, "writ account of myself." This summary of his spiritual state, written nearly a year after his shipboard self-analysis and seven months after his experience at Aldersgate, lays his spiritual quandary before the public eye, because it soon became part of his published *Journal.*

Thursday, [January] 4. One who had had the form of godliness many years wrote the following reflections:

My friends affirm I am mad, because I said I was not a Christian a year ago. I affirm I am not a Christian now. Indeed, what I might have been I know not, had I been faithful to the grace then given, when, expecting nothing less, I received such a sense of the forgiveness of my sins as till then I never knew. But that I am not a Christian at this day I as assuredly know as that Jesus is the Christ.

For a Christian is one who has the fruits of the Spirit of Christ, which (to mention no more) are love, peace, joy. But these I have not. I have not any love of God. I do not love either the Father or the Son. Do you ask how do I know whether I love God? I answer by another question, "How do you know whether you love me?" Why, as you know whether you are hot or cold. You *feel* this moment that you do or do not love me. And I *feel* this moment I do not love God; which therefore I *know* because I *feel* it. There is no word more proper, more clear, or more strong.

And I know it also by St. John's plain rule, "If any man love the world, the love of the Father is not in him." For I love the world. I desire the things of the world, some or other of them, and have done all my life. I have always placed some part of my happiness in some or other of the things that are seen. Particularly in meat and drink, and in the company of those I loved. For many years I have been, yea, and still am, hankering after a happiness in loving and being loved by one or another. And in these I have from time to time taken more pleasure than in God.

Again, joy in the Holy Ghost I have not. I have now and then some starts of joy in God. But it is not that joy. For it is not abiding. Neither is it greater than I have had on some worldly occasions. So that I can in no wise be said to "rejoice evermore," much less to "rejoice with joy unspeakable and full of glory."

Yet again, I have not "the peace of God"; *that* peace peculiarly so called. The peace I have may be accounted for on natural principles. I have health, strength, friends, a competent fortune, and a composed, cheerful temper. Who would not have a sort of peace in such circumstances? But I have none which can with any propriety be called "a peace which passeth all understanding."

From hence I conclude (and let all the *saints of the world* hear, that whereinsoever they boast they may be found even as I), though I have given, and do give, all my goods to feed the poor, I am not a Christian. Though I have endured hardship, though I have in all things denied myself and taken up my cross, I am not a Christian. My works are nothing, my sufferings are nothing; I have not the fruits of the Spirit of Christ. Though I have constantly used all the means of grace for twenty years, I am not a Christian.

CHAPTER 6

THE EXTRA-PAROCHIAL PREACHER

The year 1739 is a watershed in Wesley's spiritual and vocational self-understanding. His religious struggles of the previous years had brought him to a point where his personal affirmation of faith was accompanied by a personal assurance of faith. What was lacking in his continuing trial of spirit was any constant sense of confidence in his salvation and any strong public affirmation of the authenticity of his faith. He was now barred from preaching in many of the pulpits he had frequently occupied. The Moravians, who had helped him take some of the crucial steps in his spiritual pilgrimage, spurned him from the Lord's Table while he was visiting them in Germany. To them, he seemed still to be *homo perturbatus* (a troubled person), because he did not exhibit that sure sense of confidence and joy they felt was a necessary mark of a valid faith. Even his rediscovery in the fall of 1738 that the Homilies of the Church of England outlined the precise understanding of salvation that he had been formulating for at least a decade was not fully satisfying; the faith described therein—a sure trust and confidence—still seemed in many ways to elude him.

A crucial turning point seems to have occurred in early April 1739, when he moved from a somewhat personal and parochial sort of ministry to a more public and evangelical sense of vocation. In his *Journal,* Wesley introduced what he called "this new period of my life" by reprinting a letter he had written to his father in 1734 (see above, page 72). In it he had explained that his decision to remain at Oxford was based on the principle that whatever life best promoted holiness in himself would not only tend most to the glory of God but would thus also promote holiness in others. He had acknowledged at that time that the obverse might also be true. He was now about to discover that it would indeed become true in his own life and ministry.

Wesley's pastoral concerns had previously focused almost entirely on the nurturing of fellow Christians within the structure of the church. In this work, his own life of holiness was a basic and almost obsessive concern. This combination of personal and parochial concerns had marked the rise of Methodism during its first decade. Now his public mission would subsume his personal quest and would provide what affirmation was necessary for his personal stance.

The Field Preacher

The following account, later published in the *Journal,* describes the events in Bristol that turned Wesley into a public evangelist who proclaimed the grace and love of God to crowds gathered in all sorts of places. The journal account not only describes the rather amazing response of the people to this ministry (in many cases far beyond his own understanding or comfort), but also tries to explain his own rationale for entering into these activities. A letter inserted into the text (probably to John Clayton, an early Methodist at Oxford) presents his classic defense of his adopted method of spreading scriptural holiness: itinerant preaching. Since Wesley's collegiate ordination was not to any single parish, he was not limited by any parish boundaries, but rather he saw "the whole world" as his parish.

["This new period of my life," 1739.]
Saturday, [March] 31. In the evening I reached Bristol and met Mr. Whitefield there. I could scarce reconcile myself at first to this

John Wesley M.A.

Ætatis 63.

Wesley chose this engraving by Bland of a painting by Nathaniel Hone, R.A. (1718–84), to be the frontispiece of his *Explanatory Notes Upon the Old Testament* (1765). The engraver smoothed out many wrinkles evident in the painting and made Wesley appear much younger than the 63 years of age indicated by the caption.

strange way of preaching in the fields, of which he set me an example on Sunday, having been all my life (till very lately) so tenacious of every point relating to decency and order, that I should have thought the saving of souls almost a sin if it had not been done in a church.

April 1. In the evening (Mr. Whitefield being gone) I began expounding our Lord's Sermon on the Mount (one pretty remarkable precedent of field-preaching, though I suppose there were churches at that time also) to a little society which was accustomed to meet once or twice a week in Nicholas Street.

Monday 2. At four in the afternoon, I submitted to be more vile and proclaimed in the highways the glad tidings of salvation, speaking from a little eminence in a ground adjoining to the city to about three thousand people. The scripture on which I spoke was this (is it possible anyone should be ignorant that it is fulfilled in every true minister of Christ?), "The Spirit of the Lord is upon me, because he hath anointed me to preach the gospel to the poor. He hath sent me to heal the brokenhearted; to preach deliverance to the captives and recovery of sight to the blind; to set at liberty them that are bruised, to proclaim the acceptable year of the Lord."

At seven I began expounding the Acts of the Apostles to a society meeting in Baldwin Street, and the next day the Gospel of St. John in the chapel at Newgate, where I also daily read the Morning Service of the Church.

Wednesday 4. At Baptist Mills (a sort of a suburb or village about half a mile from Bristol), I offered the grace of God to about fifteen hundred persons from these words, "I will heal their backsliding, I will love them freely."

In the evening three women agreed to meet together weekly with the same intention as those at London, viz., "To confess their faults one to another and pray one for another that they may be healed." At eight, four young men agreed to meet in pursuance of the same design. How dare any man deny this to be (as to the substance of it) a means of grace, ordained by God? Unless he will affirm (with Luther in the fury of his Solifidianism) that St. James's Epistle is an epistle of straw. . . .

Sunday 29. I declared the free grace of God to about four thousand people from those words, "He that spared not his own Son, but delivered him up for us all, how shall he not with him also freely give us all things?'' At that hour it was that one who had long continued in sin, from a despair of finding mercy, received a full, clear sense of his pardoning love and power to sin no more. I then went to Clifton, a mile from Bristol, at the minister's desire, who was dangerously ill, and thence returned to a little plain near Hannam Mount, where about three thousand were present. After dinner I went to Clifton again. The church was quite full at the prayers and sermon, as was the churchyard at the burial which followed. From Clifton we went to Rose Green where were, by computation, near seven thousand, and thence to Gloucester Lane society. After which was our first love feast in Baldwin Street. O how had God renewed my strength! who used ten years ago to be so faint and weary with preaching *twice* in one day!

Monday 30. We understood that many were offended at the cries of those on whom the power of God came; among whom was a physician who was much afraid there might be fraud or imposture in the case. Today one whom he had known many years was the first (while I was preaching in Newgate) who broke out ''into strong cries and tears.'' He could hardly believe his own eyes and ears. He went and stood close to her and observed every symptom, till great drops of sweat ran down her face and all her bones shook. He then knew not what to think, being clearly convinced it was not fraud, nor yet any natural disorder. But when both her soul and body were healed in a moment, he acknowledged the finger of God. . . .

Monday, [May] 7. I was preparing to set out for Pensford, having now had leave to preach in the church, when I received the following note:

''Sir, our minister, having been informed you are beside yourself, does not care you should preach in any of his churches.''

I went, however, and on Priest Down, about half a mile from Pensford, preached Christ our ''wisdom, righteousness, sanctification, and redemption.''

Tuesday 8. I went to Bath, but was not suffered to be in the meadow where I was before, which occasioned the offer of a much more convenient place, where I preached Christ to about a thousand souls.

Wednesday 9. We took possession of a piece of ground near St.

James's churchyard in the Horse Fair, where it was designed to build a room large enough to contain both the societies of Nicholas and Baldwin Street, and such of their acquaintance as might desire to be present with them at such times as the Scripture was expounded. And on Saturday, 12, the first stone was laid, with the voice of praise and thanksgiving.

I had not at first the least apprehension or design of being personally engaged, either in the expense of this work or in the direction of it, having appointed eleven feoffees on whom I supposed these burdens would fall of course. But I quickly found my mistake; first with regard to the expense, for the whole undertaking must have stood still had not I immediately taken upon myself the payment of all the workmen, so that before I knew where I was, I had contracted a debt of more than a hundred and fifty pounds. And this I was to discharge how I could, the subscriptions of both societies not amounting to one quarter of the sum. And as to the direction of the work, I presently received letters from my friends in London, Mr. Whitefield in particular, backed with a message by one just come from thence, that neither he nor they would have any thing to do with the building, neither contribute anything towards it, unless I would instantly discharge all feoffees and do everything in my own name. Many reasons they gave for this, but one was enough, viz., "that such feoffees always would have it in their power to control me, and if I preached not as they like, to turn me out of the room I had built." I accordingly yielded to their advice, and calling all the feoffees together, cancelled (no man opposing) the instrument made before, and took the whole management into my own hands. Money, it is true, I had not, nor any human prospect or probability of procuring it; but I knew "the earth is the Lord's and the fullness thereof," and in his name set out, nothing doubting. . . .

My ordinary employment in public was now as follows: every morning I read prayers and preached at Newgate. Every evening I expounded a portion of Scripture at one or more of the societies. On Monday, in the afternoon, I preached abroad near Bristol; on Tuesday, at Bath and Two-Mile-Hill alternately; on Wednesday, at Baptist Mills; every other Thursday, near Pensford; every other Friday, in another part of Kingswood; on Saturday, in the afternoon, and Sunday morning, in the Bowling Green (which lies near the middle of the city); on Sunday, at eleven, near Hannam Mount; at two, at Clifton; and at five on Rose Green; and hitherto, as my days, so my strength hath been. . . .

During this whole time I was almost continually asked, either by those who purposely came to Bristol to inquire concerning this strange work, or by my old or new correspondents, "How can these things be?" And innumerable cautions were given me (generally grounded on gross misrepresentations of things) not to regard visions or dreams or to fancy people had remission of sins because of their cries, or tears, or bare outward professions. To one who had many times wrote to me on this head, the sum of my answer was as follows:

> The question between us turns chiefly, if not wholly, on matter of fact. You deny that God does now work these effects; at least, that he works them in this manner. I affirm both, because I have heard these things with my own ears and have seen them with my eyes. I have seen (as far as a thing of this kind can be seen) very many persons changed in a moment from the spirit of fear, horror, despair, to the spirit of love, joy, and peace, and from sinful desire, till then reigning over them, to a pure desire of doing the will of God. . . . I will show you him that was a lion till then, and is now a lamb; him that was a drunkard, and is now exemplarily sober; the whoremonger that was, who now abhors the very "garment spotted by the flesh." These are my living arguments for what I assert, viz., "That God does now, as aforetime, give remission of sins and the gift of the Holy Ghost, even to us and to our children; yea, and that always suddenly, as far as I have known, and often in dreams or in the visions of God." If it be not so, I am found a false witness before God. For these things I *do,* and by his grace *will,* testify.

. . . Yet many would not believe. They could not indeed *deny* the facts, but they could *explain* them away. Some said, "These were purely *natural* effects; the people fainted away only because of the heat and closeness of the rooms." And others were "sure it was all a cheat; they might help it if they would. Else why were these things only in their private societies; why were they not done in the face of the sun?" Today, Monday 21, our Lord answered for himself. For while I was enforcing these words, "Be still, and know that I am God," He began to make bare his arm, not in a close room, neither in private, but in the open air and before more than two thousands witnesses. One, and another, and another was struck to the earth, exceedingly trembling at the presence of His power. Others cried with a loud and bitter cry, "What must we do to be saved?" And in less than an hour seven persons, wholly unknown to me till that time, were rejoicing and singing, and with all their might giving thanks to the God of their salvation. . . . Surely God hath yet a work to do in this place. I have not found such love, no, not in England; nor so child-like, artless, teachable a temper, as He hath given to this people.

Yet during this whole time, I had many thoughts concerning the unusual manner of my ministering among them. But after frequently laying it before the Lord and calmly weighing whatever objections I heard against it, I could not but adhere to what I had some time since wrote to a friend who had freely spoken his sentiments concerning it. An extract of that letter I here subjoin, that the matter may be placed in a clear light.

Dear Sir,

The best return I can make for the kind freedom you use is to use the same to you. O may the God whom we serve sanctify it to us both and teach us the whole truth as it is in Jesus!

You say you cannot reconcile some parts of my behaviour with the character I have long supported. No, nor ever will. Therefore I have disclaimed that character on every possible occasion. I told all in our ship, all at Savannah, all at Frederica, and that over and over, in express terms, "I am not a Christian; I only follow after, if haply I may attain it." When they urged my works and self-denial, I answered short, "Though I give all my goods to feed the poor and my body to be burned, I am nothing, for I have not charity; I do not love God with all my heart." If they added, "Nay, but you could not preach as you do if you was not a Christian," I again confronted them with St. Paul: "Though I speak with the tongues of men and angels, and have not charity, I am nothing." Most earnestly, therefore, both in public and private, did I inculcate this: "Be not ye shaken, however I may fall, for the foundation standeth sure."

If you ask on what principle, then, I acted, it was this: "A desire to be a Christian, and a conviction that whatever I judge conducive thereto, that I am bound to do; wherever I judge I can best answer this end, thither it is my duty to go." On this principle I set out for America; on this I visited the Moravian Church; and on the same am I ready now (God being my helper) to go to Abyssinia or China or whithersoever it shall please God by this conviction to call me.

As to your advice that I should settle in College, I have no business there, having now no office and no pupils. And whether the other branch of your proposal be expedient for me, viz., "To accept of a cure of souls," it will be time enough to consider when one is offered to me.

But in the meantime you think I ought to sit still because otherwise I should invade another's office if I interfered with other people's business and intermeddled with souls that did not belong to me. You accordingly ask, "How is it that I assemble Christians who are none of my charge, to sing psalms, and pray, and hear the scriptures expounded?" and think it hard to justify doing this in other men's parishes, upon Catholic principles.

Permit me to speak plainly. If by Catholic principles you mean any other than scriptural, they weigh nothing with me; I allow no other rule, whether of faith or practice, than the Holy Scriptures; but on scriptural principles, I do not think it hard to justify whatever I do. God in scripture commands me, according to my power, to instruct the ignorant, reform the wicked, confirm the virtuous. Man forbids me to do this in another's parish; that is, in effect, to do it at all, seeing I have now no parish of my own nor probably ever shall. Whom then shall I hear, God or man? "If it be just to obey man rather than God, judge you. A dispensation of the gospel is committed to me, and woe is me if I preach not the gospel." But where shall I preach it, upon the principles you mention? Why, not in Europe, Asia, Africa, or America; not in any of the Christian parts, at least, of the habitable earth. For all these are, after a sort, divided into parishes. If it be said, "Go back, then, to the heathens from whence you came," nay, but neither could I now (on your principles) preach to them, for all the heathens in Georgia belong to the parish either of Savannah or Frederica.

Suffer me now to tell you my principles in this matter. I look upon all the world as my parish; thus far I mean, that in whatever part of it I am, I judge it meet, right, and my bounden duty to declare unto all that are willing to hear, the glad tidings of salvation. This is the work which I know God has called me to, and sure I am that his blessing attends it. Great encouragement have I, therefore, to be faithful in fulfilling the work He hath given me to do. His servant I am and, as such, am employed according to the plain direction of his word, "As I have opportunity, doing good unto all men." And his providence clearly concurs with his word; which has disengaged me from all things else that I might singly attend on this very thing, "and go about doing good."

If you ask, "How can this be? How can one do good of whom men say all manner of evil?" I will put you in mind (though you once knew this, yea, and much established me in that great truth), the more evil men say of me for my Lord's sake, the more good will He do by me. . . . Blessed be God, I enjoy the reproach of Christ! O may you also be vile, exceedingly vile for his sake! God forbid that you should ever be other than generally scandalous; I had almost said universally. If any man tell you there is a new way of following Christ, "he is a liar and the truth is not in him."

I am, etc.

Wednesday, [June] 13. In the morning I came to London, and after receiving the Holy Communion at Islington, I had once more an opportunity of seeing my mother, whom I had not seen since my return from Germany.

I cannot but mention an odd circumstance here. I had read her a paper in June last year containing a short account of what had passed in my own soul till within a few days of that time. She greatly approved it and said she heartily blessed God, who had brought me to so just a way of thinking. While I was in Germany, a copy of that paper was sent (without my knowledge) to one of my relations. He sent an account of it to my mother, whom I now found under strange fears concerning me, being convinced "by an account taken from one of my own papers, that I had greatly erred from the faith." I could not conceive what paper that should be;

but on inquiry found it was the same I had read her myself. How hard is it to form a true judgment of any person or thing from the account of a prejudiced relater! yea, though he be ever so honest a man—for he who gave this relation was one of unquestionable veracity. And yet by his *sincere* account of a writing which lay before his eyes, was the truth so totally disguised, that my mother knew not the paper she had heard from end to end, nor I that I had myself wrote.

The Itinerant Preacher

Though itinerant preaching was not illegal, it was quite irregular within the highly refined parochial system of the Church of England. Consequently, Wesley was invited by the Bishop of Bristol to explain his actions. The interview, which took place on August 16, 1739, brought forth from Wesley a carefully worded explanation. It was not published in his *Journal,* but is here transcribed from his own manuscript narrative of the encounter.

[Butler] Mr. Wesley, I will deal plainly with you. I once thought Mr. Whitefield and you well-meaning men. But I can't think so now. For I have heard more of you—matters of fact, sir. And Mr. Whitefield says in his *Journal,* "There are promises still to be fulfilled in me." Sir, the pretending to extraordinary revelations and gifts of the Holy Ghost is a horrid thing, a very horrid thing.

[Wesley] My Lord, for what Mr. Whitefield says, Mr. Whitefield and not I is accountable. I pretend to no extraordinary revelations or gifts of the Holy Ghost, none but what every Christian may receive and ought to expect and pray for. But I do not wonder your lordship has heard facts asserted which, if true, would prove the contrary. Nor do I wonder that your lordship, believing them true, should alter the opinion you once had of me. A quarter of an hour I spent with your lordship before, and about an hour now. And perhaps you have never conversed one other hour with anyone who spoke in my favour. But how many with those who spoke on the other side? So that your lordship could not but think as you do.

But pray, my lord, what are those facts you have heard?

[Butler] I hear you administer the Sacrament in your societies.

[Wesley] My lord, I never did yet, and I believe never shall.

[Butler] I hear, too, many people fall into fits in your societies and that you pray over them.

[Wesley] I do so, my lord. When any show by strong cries and tears that their soul is in deep anguish, I frequently pray to God to deliver them from it, and our prayer is often answered in that hour.

[Butler] Very extraordinary indeed! Well, sir, since you ask my advice, I will give it you very freely. You have no business here. You are not commissioned to preach in this diocese. Therefore I advise you to go hence.

[Wesley] My lord, my business on earth is to do what good I can. Wherever therefore I think I can do most good, there must I stay, so long as I think so. At present I think I can do most good here. Therefore here I stay.

As to my preaching here, a dispensation of the gospel is committed to me, and woe is me if I preach not the gospel wheresoever I am in the habitable world. Your lordship knows, being ordained a priest, by the commission then received, I am a priest of the Church universal. And being ordained as Fellow of a College, I was not limited to any particular cure, but have an indeterminate commission to preach the Word of God to any part of the Church of England.

I do not therefore conceive that in preaching here by this commission, I break any human law. When I am convinced I do, then it will be time to ask, "Shall I obey God or man?" But if I should be convinced in the meanwhile that I could advance the glory of God and the salvation of souls in any other place more than in Bristol and the parts adjoining, in that hour, by God's help, I will go hence, which till then I may not do.

CHAPTER 7

APOLOGIST AND PROPAGANDIST

John Wesley has often been credited as being the prime instigator of the Evangelical Revival in England. Though his cumulative influence over the whole of the eighteenth century gives some weight to this claim, we should remember that the most noticeable figure during the early years of the Revival was George Whitefield. When pamphlets appeared on the streets of London and Bristol in the 1730s attacking the Methodists, the barbs were usually aimed at Whitefield, not Wesley. Whitefield was the more popular public figure; the crowds who came to hear him preach were enthralled as much by the theatrics of his performance as by the content of his message. He gave life to the image of an "enthusiast."

Wesley began to attract the attention of the opposition only after he had followed in several of the footsteps of Whitefield—first of all, preaching to crowds in the open air, as we saw in the last section, and second, publishing extracts from his journal as a means of both advertisement and apology.

Purposeful Journalist

The occasion for Wesley's decision to publish an account of his activities came in the spring of 1740. Robert Williams, who had served on the grand jury in Savannah that had indicted Wesley, printed a broadside in Bristol, spreading before the public his account of Wesley's legal problems in Georgia, doing his best to discredit the budding new evangelist in the eyes of the public (see volume 2, page 55). Wesley decided the time had come for him to present the public with an "extract" from his journal so that his side of the Georgia story might be heard. In the process of preparing the material for the press, he decided also to include an account of the beginnings of Methodism at Oxford. The "Morgan letter" (see above, page 64) served this purpose.

A second extract closely followed the first and brought the story into the year 1738. The prefaces for each extract explain Wesley's purposes in publishing this material.

An Extract of the Rev. Mr. John Wesley's Journal,
from his Embarking for Georgia
to his Return to London (1740).

The Preface

1. It was in pursuance of an advice given by Bishop Taylor in his *Rules for Holy Living and Dying* that about fifteen years ago I began to take a more exact account than I had done before of the manner wherein I spent my time, writing down how I had employed every hour. This I continued to do, wherever I was, till the time of my leaving England. The variety of scenes which I then passed through induced me to transcribe from time to time the more material parts of my diary, adding here and there such little reflections as occurred to my mind. Of this journal thus occasionally compiled, the following is a short extract, it not being my design to relate all those particulars which I wrote for my own use only and which would answer no valuable end to others, however important they were to me.

2. Indeed I had no design or desire to trouble the world with any of my little affairs, as can't but appear to every impartial mind from my having been so long "as one that heareth not," notwithstanding the loud and frequent calls I have had to answer for myself. Neither should I have done it now had not Captain Williams' affidavit, published as soon as he had left England, laid

an obligation upon me to do what in me lies, in obedience to that command of God, "Let not the good which is in you be evil-spoken of." With this view I do at length give an answer to every man that asketh me a reason of the hope which is in me, that in all these things I have a conscience void of offence, towards God and towards man.

3. I have prefixed hereto a letter wrote several years since, containing a plain account of the rise of that little society in Oxford which has been so variously represented. Part of this was published in 1733, but without my consent or knowledge. It now stands as it was wrote, without any addition, diminution, or amendment, it being my only concern herein nakedly to declare the thing as it is.

4. Perhaps my employments of another kind may not allow me to give any farther answer to them who say all manner of evil of me falsely and seem to think that they do God service. Suffice it that both they and I shall shortly give an account to him that is ready to judge the quick and the dead.

[Extract II]

The Preface

3. What I design in the following extract is, openly to declare to all mankind what it is that the Methodists (so called) have done and are doing now, or rather, what it is that God hath done and is still doing in our land. For it is not the work of man which hath lately appeared. All who calmly observe it must say, "This is the Lord's doing and it is marvelous in our eyes." . . .

7. Yet I know even this will by no means satisfy the far greater part of those who are now offended. And for a plain reason— because they will never read it; they are resolved to hear one side, and one only. I know also that many who *do* read it will be just of the same mind they were before because they have fixed their judgment already and do not regard anything which such a fellow can say. Let them see to that. I have done my part. I have delivered mine own soul. Nay, I know that many will be greatly offended at this very account. It must be so from the very nature of things which are therein related. And the best appellation I expect from them is that of a fool, a madman, an enthusiast. All that in me

lies is to relate simple truth in as inoffensive a manner as I can. Let God give it the effect which pleaseth him and which is most for his glory!

Public Defendant

Captain Williams' broadside (see volume 2, page 56) was reprinted in the summer of 1741 after the first two portions of Wesley's *Journal* had been published. Wesley responded by selecting from his first *Journal* twelve pages of material that answered Williams' charges and publishing them separately as a small tract in September 1741. His efforts did not lay the problem to rest, however. The following summer yet another reprint of the Williams broadside appeared, which Wesley answered directly in a letter to Williams in July 1742, specifically refuting the charges in the broadside and repeating (for the third time in print) the minority report of the Savannah Grand Jury, which had defended Wesley. This letter was also published as a broadside and circulated among the public.

A Letter from the Rev. Mr. John Wesley
to Capt. Robert Williams,
occasioned by an affidavit made some time since
and lately reprinted.

Sir,

To prove that Robert Williams "traded very largely during the time he was at Savannah," that "he built very considerable buildings both at Savannah and other parts of the colony," that he "greatly improved large tracts of land there, and was esteemed to have one of the chief settlements in the colony," you have not so much as quoted "common fame." So he that *will* believe it, let him believe it.

But you have quoted "common fame" to support several charges against John Wesley, Clerk; as, that "he seduced the common persons settled there to idleness," that "he used too great familiarities with Mrs. Hopkey and continued so to do till she was married to Mr. William Williamson of Savannah, a gentleman of considerable note there" ('tis much "a gentleman of so considerable note" as Mr. William Williamson would marry her!), that "he sent her several letters and messages after her marriage, desiring her to meet him at divers unseasonable hours and places, many of which" (hours or places?) "were at his, the said Wesley's own closet." "A report was," you say, that "these things were so." Would any man desire better proof?

I am not surprised at all that upon *such* evidence you should advance *such* assertions. But I really am, at what you afterwards assert, as upon your own personal knowledge, viz., that "two bills of indictment being preferred against John Wesley and sent to the Grand Jury of Savannah" (bills of indictment *sent* to the Grand Jury! what kind of proceeding is this?) "this deponent and the rest of the Grand Jury did *unanimously* agree to the said bills." How dare you, sir, assert so gross a falsehood? Have you *no* regard either for your reputation or your soul? Do you think there is no God to judge the earth? You know, you *must* know, how large a part of that Grand Jury did absolutely disagree to every bill of the two presentments, and gave those reasons of their disagreement to the Trustees, which neither you nor any man has yet chose to answer. You assert farther that I "was bailed by two freeholders of Savannah for my appearance at the then next sessions." Here I charge you with a second, gross, willful falsehood. You know I never was bailed at all. If I was, name the men (Henry Lloyd is ready to confront you) or produce an attested copy of the record of court. You assert, thirdly, that "a little before the sessions came on" (viz., the next sessions after those bills were found) "I deserted my bail." Here is another gross, willful, palpable untruth. For (1) no bail was ever given, (2) I appeared at seven sessions successively after those bills were found, viz., on Thursday, Sept. 1, on Friday, Sept. 2, at three other sessions held in September and October, on Thursday, November 2, and lastly on Thursday, Nov. 22. (Your smaller falsehood, as that I "quitted the colony about the middle of the night," that "from Purrysburg to Charleston is about two hundred miles" [you should have said about ninety], that "I walked on foot from thence to Charlestown,"

I pass over as not material.) You lastly assert, "that the justices threatened to prosecute and imprison my bail for such his desertion, who were in the utmost confusion concerning the same. But by the interposition of this deponent and several others on behalf of the said bail, and to prevent destruction to *their* respective families, the justices respited their recognizances during pleasure."

And this is altogether fit to crown the whole. Now, sir, as you know in your own soul that every word of this is pure invention, without one grain of truth from the beginning of it to the end; what amends can you ever make, either to God or to me or to the world? Into what a dreadful dilemma have you here brought yourself? You must either openly retract an open slander or you must wade through thick and thin to support it; till that God, to whom I appeal, shall maintain his own cause and sweep you away from the earth.

I am, sir, your friend,
John Wesley.

N.B.   This was written July 16, but I had not leisure to transcribe it before August 3, 1742.

Touching some of the particulars above-mentioned, for the satisfaction of all calm and impartial men, I have added a short extract from the larger account which was published some years ago.

On Monday, August 22, Mr. Causton, then the Chief Magistrate of Savannah (having before told me himself, "I have drawn the sword and will never sheath it till I have satisfaction"), delivered to an extraordinary Grand Jury which he had summoned to meet there, a paper entitled, "A List of Grievances, presented by the Grand Jury for Savannah, this —— day of August, 1737."

This the majority of the Grand Jury altered in some particulars, and on Thursday, Sept. 1, delivered it again to the Court under the form of two presentments, containing ten bills, which were then read to the people.

Herein they asserted upon oath, "That John Wesley, Clerk, had broken the laws of the realm, contrary to the peace of our Sovereign Lord the King, his Crown and Dignity.

1. By speaking and writing to Mrs. Williamson, against her husband's consent;

2. By repelling her from the Holy Communion;

3. By not declaring his adherence to the Church of England;

4. By dividing the Morning Service on Sundays;

5. By refusing to baptize Mr. Parker's child otherwise than by dipping, except the parents would certify it was weak and not able to bear it;

6. By repelling Mr. Gough from the Holy Communion;

7. By refusing to read the Burial Service over the body of Nathaniel Polhill;

8. By calling himself Ordinary of Savannah;

9. By refusing to receive William Aglionby as a Godfather, only because he was not a communicant;

10. By refusing Jacob Matthews for the same reason, and baptizing an Indian trader's child with only two sponsors" (this I own was wrong, for I ought at all hazards to have refused baptizing it 'till he had procured a third).

The sense of the minority of the Grand Jurors concerning these presentments may appear from the following paper, which they transmitted to the Trustees:

To the Honourable the Trustees for Georgia. "Whereas two presentments have been made for the Town and County of Savannah in Georgia, against John Wesley, Clerk, —we whose names are underwritten, being members of the said Grand Jury, do humbly beg leave to signify our dislike of the said presentments, and give the reasons of our dissent from the particular bills.

With regard to the first bill, we do not apprehend that Mr. Wesley acted against any law by writing or speaking to Mrs. Williamson, since it does not appear to us that the said Mr. Wesley has either spoke in private or wrote to the said Mrs. Williamson since March [12] (the day of her marriage) except one letter of July the 5th, which he wrote at the request of her aunt, as a pastor, to exhort and reprove her.

The second we do not apprehend to be a true bill because we humbly conceive Mr. Wesley did not assume to himself any authority contrary to law; for we understand, 'every person intending to communicate should signify his name to the Curate at least some time the day before,' which Mrs. Williamson did not do, although Mr. Wesley had often in full congregation declared he did insist on a compliance with that rubric and had before repelled divers persons for non-compliance therewith.

The third we do not think a true bill because several of us have been his hearers when he has declared his adherence to the Church of England in a stronger manner than by a formal declaration, by explaining and defending the Apostles, the Nicene, and the Athanasian Creeds, the Thirty-Nine Articles, the whole Book of Common Prayer, and the Homilies of the said Church; and because we think a formal declaration is not required but from those who have received Institution and Induction.

The fact alleged in the fourth bill we cannot apprehend to be contrary to any law in being.

The fifth we do not think a true bill because we conceive Mr. Wesley is justified by the rubric, viz., 'If they (the Parents) certify that the child is weak it shall suffice to pour water upon it.' Intimating, as we humbly suppose, it shall not suffice if they do not certify.

The sixth cannot be a true bill because the said William Gough, being one of our members, was surprised to hear himself named, without his knowledge or privity, and did publicly declare, 'It was no grievance to him because the said John Wesley had given him reasons with which he was satisfied.'

The seventh we do not apprehend to be a true bill, for Mr. Nathaniel Polhill was an Anabaptist and desired in his lifetime that he might not be interred with the office of the Church of England. And farther we have good reason to believe that Mr. Wesley was at Frederica, or on his return thence, when Polhill was buried.

As to the eighth bill we are in doubt, as not well knowing the meaning of the word 'Ordinary.' But for the ninth and tenth we think Mr. Wesley is sufficiently justified by the Canons of the Church, which forbid 'any person to be admitted Godfather or Godmother to any child before the said person has received the Holy Communion,' whereas William Aglionby and Jacob Matthews had never certified Mr. Wesley that they had received it."

This was signed by twelve of the Grand Jurors of whom three were constables and six more tithingmen; who consequently would have made a majority, had the jury consisted, as it ought to have done, of only fifteen members, viz., the four constables and eleven tithingmen.

CHAPTER 8

THE PERSECUTED PREACHER

Wesley's early journals give the impression that he spent much of his time and effort coping with the physical as well as the literary attacks being made upon him. His preaching was as likely to bring riots among some people as it was to bring repentance among others. Parsons and parishioners who disliked Wesley's intrusions into their parishes found numerous ways to make his life uncomfortable, such as ringing the church bells to drown out his voice, tossing rocks and eggs at his head, or driving cows through his outdoor congregations.

Wesley's usual public response, as seen in the first selection below, was to go on about his business as much as possible, assuming that the true Christian must expect to face persecution and, therefore, must simply trust in God's providential care (see also above, page 72). This attitude did not, however, deter him from seeking legal counsel or even from threatening legal action at times to protect his individual liberties as a citizen, as the second selection below illustrates.

Providentially Protected Person

When Wesley visited Wednesbury in October 1743, he discovered that the once friendly vicar, Edward Egginton, had since April been advising the people to "drive these fellows [Methodists] out of the country." This area, just outside Birmingham, was full of rough and ready folk willing to take justice into their own hands if the justice of the peace would not oblige them. Wesley's account of the rioting on this particular visit is remarkable for its explicit analysis of the manner in which he saw the providence of God demonstrated in these events. The tone as well as the content of the narrative is significant and lends firsthand support to the growing idea that Wesley's ministry had the stamp of divine authority, just as his person had the protection of divine providence. That Wesley saw himself in the same light as the martyrs can be seen in his brother Charles' account of these events (see volume 2, pages 72-73).

The following account of the Wednesbury riot is taken from Wesley's *Journal.* He also published a version of this narrative as part of a tract entitled *Modern Christianity Exemplified at Wednesbury* (1744).

Thursday, 20 [October]. After preaching to a small, attentive congregation, I rode to Wednesbury. At twelve I preached in a ground near the middle of the town to a far larger congregation than was expected, on "Jesus Christ, the same yesterday, and today, and forever." I believe every one present felt the power of God, and no creature offered to molest us, either going or coming; but the Lord fought for us and we held our peace.

I was writing at Francis Ward's in the afternoon when the cry arose that the mob had beset the house. We prayed that God would disperse them, and it was so. One went this way and another that, so that in half an hour not a man was left. I told our brethren, "Now is the time for us to go," but they pressed me exceedingly to stay; so, that I might not offend them, I sat down, though I foresaw what would follow. Before five the mob surrounded the house again in greater numbers than ever. The cry of one and all was, "Bring out the minister; we will have the minister." I desired one to take their captain by the hand and bring him into the house. After a few sentences interchanged between us the lion was become a lamb. I desired him to go and bring one or two more of the most angry of his companions. He brought in two, who were ready to swallow the ground with rage; but in two minutes they were as calm as he. I then bade them make way, that I might go out among the people. As soon as I was in the midst of them I called for a chair and, standing up, asked, "What do any of you want with me?" Some said, "We want you to go with us to the Justice." I replied, "That I will, with all my heart." I then spoke a few words, which God applied, so that they cried out with might and main, "The gentleman is an honest gentleman, and we will spill our blood in his defence." I asked, "Shall we go to the Justice tonight, or in the morning?" Most of them cried, "Tonight, tonight," on which I went before, and two or three hundred followed, the rest returning whence they came.

The night came on before we had walked a mile, together with heavy rain. However, on we went to Bentley Hall, two miles from Wednesbury. One or two ran before to tell Mr. Lane they had brought Mr. Wesley before his Worship. Mr. Lane replied, "What have I to do with Mr. Wesley? Go and carry him back again." By this time the main body came up and began knocking at the door. A servant told them Mr. Lane was in bed. His son followed and asked what was the matter. One replied, "Why an't please you, they sing psalms all day, nay, and make folks rise at five in the morning. And what would your Worship advise us to do?" "To go home," said Mr. Lane, "and be quiet."

Here they were at a full stop, till one advised to go to Justice Persehouse at Walsall. All agreed to this, so we hastened on, and about seven came to his house. But Mr. Persehouse likewise sent word that he was in bed. Now they were at a stand again, but at last they all thought it the wisest course to make the best of their way home. About fifty of them undertook to convoy me. But we had not gone a hundred yards when the mob of Walsall came, pouring in like a flood, and bore down all before them. The Darlaston mob made what defence they could, but they were weary as well as outnumbered, so that in a short time, many being knocked down, the rest ran away and left me in their hands.

To attempt speaking was vain, for the noise on every side was like the roaring of the sea. So they dragged me along till we came to the town, where, seeing the door of a large house open, I attempted to go in; but a man, catching me by the hair, pulled me back into the middle of the mob. They made no more stop till they had carried me through the main street, from one end of the town to the other. I continued speaking all the time to those within hearing, feeling no pain or weariness. At the west end of the town, seeing a door half open, I made toward it and would have gone in, but a gentleman in the shop would not suffer me, saying they would pull the house down to the ground. However, I stood at the door and asked, "Are you willing to hear me speak?" Many cried out, "No, no! knock his brains out; down with him; kill him at once." Others said, "Nay, but we will hear him first." I began asking, "What evil have I done? Which of you all have I wronged in word or deed?" and continued speaking for above a quarter of an hour, till my voice suddenly failed. Then the floods began to lift up their voice again, many crying out, "Bring him away! Bring him away!"

In the meantime my strength and my voice returned and I broke out aloud into prayer. And now the man who just before headed the mob turned and said, "Sir, I will spend my life for you; follow me and not one soul here shall touch a hair of your head." Two or three of his fellows confirmed his words and got close to me immediately. At the same time, the gentleman in the shop cried out, "For shame, for shame! Let him go." An honest butcher, who was a little farther off, said it was a shame they should do thus, and pulled back four or five, one after another, who were running on the most fiercely. The people then, as if it had been by common consent, fell back to the right and left, while those three or four men took me between them and carried me through them all. But on the bridge the mob rallied again. We therefore went on one side over the mill-dam and thence through the meadows till, a little before ten, God brought me safe to Wednesbury, having lost only one flap of my waistcoat and a little skin from one of my hands.

I never saw such a chain of providences before—so many convincing proofs that the hand of God is on every person and thing, overruling all as it seemeth Him good.

The poor woman of Darlaston who had headed that mob and sworn that none should touch me, when she saw her followers give way, ran into the thickest of the throng and knocked down three or four men, one after another. But many assaulting her at once, she was soon overpowered, and had probably been killed in a few minutes (three men keeping her down and beating her with all their might) had not a man called to one of them, "Hold, Tom, hold!" "Who is there?" said Tom. "What, honest Munchin? Nay, then, let her go." So they held their hand, and let her get up and crawl home as well as she could.

From the beginning to the end I found the same presence of mind as if I had been sitting in my own study. But I took no thought for one moment before another; only once it came into my mind that, if they should throw me into the river, it would spoil the papers that were in my pocket. For myself, I did not doubt that I should swim across, having but a thin coat and a light pair of boots.

The circumstances which follow, I thought, were particularly remarkable: (1) That many endeavoured to throw me down while we were going downhill on a slippery path to the town, as well judging, that if I was once on the ground, I should hardly rise any more. But I made no stumble at all, nor the least slip till I was entirely out of their hands. (2) That although many strove to lay hold on my collar or clothes to pull me down, they could not fasten at all; only one got fast hold of the flap of my waistcoat, which was soon left in his hand; the other flap, in the pocket of which was a bank-note, was torn but held off. (3) That a lusty man just behind struck at me several times with a large oaken stick, with which, if he had struck me once on the back part of my head, it would have saved him all farther trouble. But every time the blow was turned aside, I know not how, for I could not move to the right hand or left. (4) That another came rushing through the press and raising his arm to strike, on a sudden let it drop and only stroked my head, saying "What soft hair he has!" (5) That I stopped exactly at the mayor's door, as if I had known it (which the mob doubtless thought I did), and found him standing in the shop, which gave the first check to the madness of the people. (6) That the very first men whose hearts were turned were the heroes of the town, the captains of the rabble on all occasions, one of them having been a prizefighter at the bear-garden. (7) That from first to last, I heard none give a reviling word or call me by any opprobrious name whatever; but the cry of one and all was, "The preacher! The preacher! The parson! The minister!" (8) That no creature, at least within my hearing, laid anything to my charge, either true or false; having in the hurry quite forgot to provide themselves with an accusation of any kind. And lastly, that they were as utterly at a loss what they should do with me, none proposing any determinate thing, only, "Away with him! Kill him at once!"

By how gentle degrees does God prepare us for His will! Two years ago a piece of brick grazed my shoulders. It was a year after that the stone struck me between the eyes. Last month I received one blow, and this evening two—one before we came into the town and one after we were gone out; but both were as nothing, for though one man struck me on the breast with all his might and the other on the mouth with such a force that the blood gushed out immediately, I felt no more pain from either of the blows than if they had touched me with a straw. . . .

When I came back to Francis Ward's I found many of our brethren waiting upon God. Many also whom I never had seen before came to rejoice with us. And the next morning, as I rode through the town on my way to Nottingham, every one I met expressed such a cordial affection that I could scarce believe what I saw and heard.

Unjustly Treated Citizen

Wesley considered the riotous opposition to his preaching to be unprovoked; he did not intentionally bring persecution upon himself. In some cases, he felt his liberties as an Englishman had been blatantly disregarded not only by the mobs but also by the authorities.

In August 1748, Wesley and some friends were attacked at Roughlee in the West Riding of Yorkshire by a mob incited to action by George White, the Anglican minister at the neighboring town of Colne (see volume 2, page 74). The Rev. Mr. White had gone so far as to issue the following notice to mobilize the anti-Wesleyan forces:

NOTICE is hereby given, that if any men be mindful to enlist into his Majesty's service under the command of the Rev. Mr. George White, commander-in-chief, and John Bannister, lieutenant-general of his Majesty's forces, for the defence of the Church of England and the support of the manufactory in and about Colne, both of which are now in danger, etc., etc., let them now repair to the Drum Head at the Cross, where each man shall have a pint of ale for advance, and other proper encouragements.

The day after the confrontation with the mob, Wesley sent the following letter to the local constable, James Hargrave, describing and protesting the "lawless violence" he had suffered under Hargrave's jurisdiction. Wesley published excerpts from the middle portion of this letter in his *Journal* account of the event; he omitted, however, the portions indicated below within brackets, including the implied threat of legal action at the end.

Sir,

[When I came last night to Roughlee I found abundance of people, many of whom pressed me to preach there; but I told them, I had given my word I would not preach there that evening. They then desired me to stay with them all night; but this also I refused, staying no longer than till our horses were ready, and till I had given them a short exhortation not to be out late at night, and as much as lay in them to live peaceably with all men.

This is a short account of what I've done. I must now mention a little what you have done. I say you, because all that was done yesterday was in the eye of the law, as much your act and deed as if you had done all with your own hands; seeing (not to touch now upon some other points, evidence of which may be produced in due time) all those actions are imputable to you which you could have prevented and would not.]

Between twelve and one o'clock, when I was speaking to some quiet people, without any noise or tumult, a drunken rabble came with clubs and staves, in a tumultuous and riotous manner, the captain of whom, Richard Bocock by name, said he was a deputy constable, and that he was come to bring me to you. I made no resistance (though he had no warrant to show, and consequently all he did was utterly illegal), but went with him. I had scarce gone ten yards when a man of his company struck me with his fist in the face, with all his might. I told him it was not well, and went on. Quickly after, another threw his stick at my head. I then made a stand, having little encouragement to go forward. But another of the champions, cursing and swearing in the most shocking manner, and flourishing his club over his head, cried out, "Bring him away!" So perceiving there was no remedy, I walked on to Barrowford (where they informed me you was), their drummer going before to draw all the rabble together and encourage them in their work.

[I must just stop to inform you (if you know it not) that the whole action of carrying me along against my will was an assault upon the king's highway, contrary to his peace, crown, and dignity.]

When your deputy had brought me prisoner into the house, he permitted Mr. Grimshaw, the minister of Haworth, Mr. Colbeck of Keighley, and one more, to be with me, promising none should hurt them. Soon after you and your friends came in and required me to promise I would "come to Roughlee no more." I told you I would "cut off my hand rather than make any such promise." Neither would I promise that none of my friends should come. After abundance of rambling discourse . . . you seemed a little satisfied with my saying, "I will not preach at Roughlee this time. Nor shall I be here again till August next. Then I will show you the authority by which I preach." You then undertook to quiet the mob, to whom you went and spoke a few words, and their noise immediately ceased, while I walked out with you at the back door.

I should have mentioned that I had desired you to let me go several times before, but could not prevail, and that when I attempted to go with Richard Bocock the mob came immediately to me, cursing and swearing and throwing whatever came to hand. One of them beat me down to the ground, and when I rose again the rest came about me like lions and forced me back into the house.

While you and I went out at one door, Mr. Grimshaw and Mr. Colbeck went out at the other. The mob immediately closed them in and tossed them to and fro with the utmost violence, threw Mr. Grimshaw down, and loaded them both with dirt and mire, not one of your friends offering to assist them or call off the bloodhounds from the pursuit. The other quiet, harmless people, which followed me at a distance to see what the end would be, they treated still worse, not only by your connivance, but by the express order of your deputy. They made them flee for their lives amidst showers of dirt and stones, without any regard to age or sex. Some of them they trampled in the mire and dragged by the hair, particularly a young man who came with me from Newcastle. Many they beat with the clubs without mercy. One they forced to leap down (or they would have cast him headlong) from a rock ten or twelve foot high into the river, and even when he crawled out, wet and bruised, they swore they would throw him in again, and he hardly escaped out of their hands.

At this time, you sat well-pleased close to the scene of action, not attempting in the least to hinder them. And all this time you was talking of justice and law. Alas! Suppose we were dissenters (which I utterly deny, consequently laws against dissenting conventicles are nothing at all to us); suppose we were Turks or Jews; still are we not to have the benefit of the law of our country? Proceed against us by law, if you can or dare, but not by lawless violence—not by making a drunken, cursing, swearing, riotous mob both judge, jury, and executioner. This is flat rebellion both against God and the king.

[But before I take any further step herein I think myself obliged to make you a fair proposal. If you will promise me under your hand to suppress all mobs at Roughlee and the parts adjacent (as your duty both to God and the king require you to do, even at the hazard of your life); if you will promise to proceed only by law against those you apprehend to act contrary to law (which indeed I absolutely deny you to do)—nor can it be supposed that none of the lawyers in Leeds, Newcastle, Bristol, or London, should find it out (if it were so), but only the Solomons in Pendle Forest [i.e. the vicinity of Roughlee]; if I accordingly find a letter from you to this effect when I come to London, directed to the Foundery near Moorfields, I shall be satisfied and proceed no further. If not, I shall try another course.

Only one piece of advice permit me to give. Do not consult herein with some petty attorney (who will certainly say your cause is good), but with some able barrister-at-law. This is the course I take. The counsel to whom I applied on this very Act of Parliament before I left London were Counsellor Glanville, a barrister of Gray's Inn, and Sir Dudley Ryder, the King's Attorney-General.

I am your real friend.]

CHAPTER 9

THE MEDICAL PRACTITIONER

Wesley never fancied himself a medical doctor, but he did exhibit a lifelong interest in the prevention and cure of disease. The earliest records of his reading at Oxford list books on health; his Georgia diary notes his participation in an autopsy in 1736; his letters contain frequent suggestions to friends regarding their physical well-being; and his *Journal* displays his continual fascination with cures and remedies.

Wesley's dipping into matters of "physic" was more than the casual preoccupation of a busy but inherently curious mind. He understood himself having a responsibility as a Christian for meeting the needs of his neighbor, whether those needs be the result of sin, poverty, ignorance, or even illness. His interest in medicine arose out of a holistic concern for persons, including their health. The focus of his interest was in prevention as well as cure. He spent little time with the *theory* of disease, but rather emphasized the practical, experimental approach to prevention and cure.

Two activities best exhibit Wesley's role as a practitioner of the medical arts. He established free medical dispensaries and published a popular collection of cures and remedies.

Dispenser of Medicine

Wesley's work among the poor increasingly confirmed his prejudices against self-serving physicians and apothecaries whom he saw conspiring to take advantage of sick persons for their own selfish gain. His direct, practical solution to the problem was to provide for the sick himself in ways he felt most appropriate to their needs.

One step was to ask members of the Methodist societies to act as "Visitors to the Sick." He assigned this small army of volunteers by pairs to designated areas of town, asking them to follow these simple rules: "(1) Be plain and open in dealing with souls. (2) Be mild, tender, patient. (3) Be cleanly in all you do for the sick. (4) Be not nice [rude]."

Wesley soon became aware of the pressing need for more direct and adequate medical assistance. He then took the rather astonishing step in 1746 of opening a medical clinic on his own in Bristol. Within a short time, he established other free public dispensaries in London and Newcastle as well. These are often said to be the first free clinics in England.

Wesley explained his rationale for these activities in a letter to his friend, the Rev. Vincent Perronet, later published as section XII of "A Plain Account of the People Called Methodists."

1. But I was still in pain for many of the poor that were sick; there was so great expense and so little profit. And first I resolved to try whether they might not receive more benefit in the hospitals. Upon the trial, we found there was indeed less expense, but no more good done than before. I then asked the advice of several physicians for them; but still it profited not. I saw the poor people pining away, and several families ruined, and that without remedy.

2. At length I thought of a kind of desperate expedient. "I will prepare and give them physic myself." For six- or seven-and-twenty years I had made anatomy and physic the diversion of my leisure hours; though I never properly studied them, unless for a few months when I was going to America, where I imagined I

might be of some service to those who had no regular physician among them. I applied to it again. I took into my assistance an apothecary and an experienced surgeon; resolving at the same time not to go out of my depth, but to leave all difficult and complicated cases to such physicians as the patients should choose.

3. I gave notice of this to the Society; telling them that all who were ill of chronical distempers (for I did not care to venture upon acute) might, if they pleased, come to me at such a time, and I would give them the best advice I could and the best medicines I had.

4. Many came (and so every Friday since); among the rest was one William Kirkham, a weaver, near Old Nichol Street. I asked him, "What complaint have you?" "O sir," said he, "a cough, a very sore cough. I can get no rest day nor night."

I asked, "How long have you had it?" He replied, "About three-score years; it began when I was eleven years old." I was nothing glad that this man should come first, fearing our not curing him might discourage others. However, I looked up to God and said, "Take this three or four times a day. If it does you no good, it will do you no harm." He took it two or three days. His cough was cured, and has not returned to this day.

5. Now, let candid men judge, does humility require me to deny a notorious fact? If not, which is vanity? to say I by my own skill restored this man to health, or to say God did it by His own almighty power? By what figure of speech this is called boasting I know not. But I will put no name to such a fact as this. I leave that to the Rev. Dr. Middleton [author of *A Free Inquiry into the Miraculous Powers which are supposed to have subsisted in the Christian Church* (1748)].

6. In five months medicines were occasionally given to above five hundred persons. Several of these I never saw before; for I did not regard whether they were of the Society or not. In that time seventy-one of these, regularly taking their medicines and following the regimen prescribed (which three in four would not do), were entirely cured of distempers long thought to be incurable. The whole expense of medicines during this time was nearly forty pounds. We continued this ever since, and by the blessing of God with more and more success.

Prescriber of Remedies

Wesley's growing notoriety as a medical practitioner became more firmly fixed in the public mind with the publication in 1747 of his *Primitive Physick; or An Easy and Natural Method of Curing Most Diseases.* This curious collection of folk remedies, "tried and true," was revised and enlarged several times, going through at least twenty-two editions in England during Wesley's lifetime. Beginning at mid-century, it was frequently republished in Ireland and America and was translated into French and Welsh before the century was out. It was the companion of many a pioneer on the American frontier well into the nineteenth century.

The popularity of this little book was explained in part by Wesley's comment in the preface—every person who owned it had "a physician always in his house, and one that attends without fee or reward." It also carried the weight of Wesley's authority and experimental *imprimatur:* those remedies he could vouch for personally, he marked "Tried"; those he felt worked best, he marked with an asterisk; and those which never failed, he claimed as "Infallible," indicated by an *"I."*

Wesley had no qualms about undercutting part of the medical profession of his day. In the preface, he explains that he is simply reviving the ancient art of healing diseases by using remedies that are known to cure the illnesses. He claims that the medical faculty had in large part lost their effectiveness as well as the trust of the public through an obscurantist fascination with the theory of diseases and a selfish desire to increase their wealth (even if it meant intentionally prolonging the plight of the poor sick). Wesley recommends that in cases of continuing or severe illness, the sick person search out a "physician who fears God." The profession struck back in the writings of William Hawes (see volume 2, page 128).

The following selections from the 1772 (15th) edition explain Wesley's understanding of his role in providing these prescriptions for health and illustrate a cross section of his suggested recipes. To the present reader, some of these may seem obvious (#117), or ridiculous (#729), or even surprisingly modern (#582).

Preface

. . . 'Tis probable, physic, as well as religion, was in the first ages chiefly traditional; every father delivering down to his sons what he had himself in like manner received concerning the manner of healing both outward hurts, with the diseases incident to each climate, and the medicines which were of the greatest efficacy for the cure of each disorder. . . . Thus ancient men, having a little experience joined with common sense and common humanity, cured both themselves and their neighbours of most of the distempers, to which every nation was subject.

But in the process of time, men of a philosophical turn were not satisfied with this. They began to enquire how they might *account* for these things? . . . And hence the whole order of physic, which had obtained to that time came gradually to be inverted. Men of learning began to set experience aside; to build physic upon hypotheses; to form theories of diseases and their cure, and to substitute these in the place of experiments . . . till at length physic became an abstruse science, quite out of the reach of ordinary men. . . .

Yet there have not been wanting from time to time, some lovers of mankind who have endeavoured (even contrary to their own interest) to reduce physic to its ancient standard: who have laboured to explode out of it all hypotheses and fine spun theories and to make it a plain intelligible thing, as it was in the beginning, having no more mystery in it than this—"Such a medicine removes such a pain." These have demonstrably shown that neither the knowledge of astrology, astronomy, natural philosophy, nor even anatomy itself, is absolutely necessary to the quick and effectual cure of most diseases incident to human bodies; nor yet any chemical, or exotic, or compound medicine, but a single plant or fruit duly applied. So that every man of common sense (unless in some rare cases) may prescribe either to himself or his neighbour, and may be very secure from doing harm, even where he can do no good.

. . . Without any concern about the obliging or disobliging any man living, a mean hand has made here some little attempt toward a plain and easy way of curing most diseases. I have only consulted herein, experience, common sense, and the common interest of mankind. And supposing they can be cured this easy way, who would desire to use any other? Who would not wish to have a physician always in his house, and one that attends without fee or reward? . . . Experience shows that one thing will cure most disorders at least as well as twenty put together. Then why do you add the other nineteen? Only to swell the Apothecary's bill; nay, possibly on purpose to prolong the distemper, that the doctor and he may divide the spoil. . . .

As to the manner of using the medicines here set down, I should advise, as soon as you know your distemper (which is very easy, unless in a complication of disorders, and then you would do well to apply to a physician that fears God), *first,* use the first of the remedies for that disease which occurs in the ensuing collection (unless some other of them be easier to be had, and then it may do just as well). *Secondly,* after a competent time, if it takes no effect, use the second, the third, and so on. I have purposely set down (in most cases) several remedies for each disorder, not only because all are not equally easy to be procured at all times and in all places, but likewise because the medicine which cures one man will not always cure another of the same distemper. Nor will it cure the same man at all times. Therefore it was necessary to have a variety. However, I have subjoined the letter *(I)* to those medicines which are thought to be *Infallible. Thirdly,* observe all the time the greatest exactness in your regimen or manner of living. Abstain from all mixed, all high-seasoned food. Use plain diet, easy of digestion, and this as sparingly as you can, consistent with ease and strength. Drink only water, if it agrees with your stomach; if not, good, clear, small beer [weak beer]. Use as much exercise daily in the open air as you can without weariness. Sup at six or seven on the lightest food. Go to bed early and rise betimes. To persevere with steadiness in this course is often more than half the cure. Above all, add to the rest (for it is not labour lost) that old unfashionable medicine, prayer. And have faith in God, who "killeth and maketh alive, who bringeth down to the grave and bringeth up." . . .

London, June 11, 1747

139

POSTSCRIPT

. . . Alterations are still in pursuance of my first design, to set down cheap, safe, and easy medicines, easy to be known, easy to be procured, and easy to be applied by plain, unlettered men. . . .

Bristol, Oct. 16, 1755

. . . I have now added the word *Tried* to those which I have found to be of the greatest efficacy. I believe many others to be of equal virtue, but it has not lain in my way to make the trial.

London, Nov. 10, 1760

.*. Most of those medicines which I prefer to the rest are now marked with an asterisk.

Oct. 20, 1772

A COLLECTION OF RECEIPTS

To cure Baldness

76. Rub the part morning and evening, with onions, till it is red; and rub it afterwards with honey.

Or, wash it with a decoction of box-wood.

Or, electrify it daily.

Blisters

104. On the feet, occasioned by walking, are cured by drawing a needle full of worsted through them. Clip it off at both ends, and leave it till the skin peels off.

Hard Breasts

109. Apply turnips roasted till soft, then mashed and mixed with a little oil of roses. Change this twice a day, keeping the breast very warm with flannel.

A Bruise

*111. Immediately apply treacle spread on brown paper: Tried.

114. Or, apply a plaister of chopped parsley mixt with butter.

To prevent Swelling from a Bruise

117. Immediately apply a cloth, five or six times doubled, dipt in cold water, and new dipt when it grows warm: Tried.

To cure a Swelling from a Bruise

118. Foment it half an hour, morning and evening, with cloths dipped in water, as hot as you can bear.

A Cold

*176. Drink a pint of cold water lying down in bed: Tried.

178. Or, to one spoonful of oatmeal, and one spoonful of honey, add a piece of butter, the bigness of a nutmeg; pour on gradually near a pint of boiling water; drink this lying down in bed.

A Cold in the Head

179. Pare very thin the yellow rind of an orange. Roll it up inside out, and thrust a roll into each nostril.

A Cough

253. Make a hole through a lemon and fill it with honey. Roast it and catch the juice. Take a tea-spoonful of this frequently: Tried.

A Cut

280. Keep it closed with your thumb a quarter of an hour. Then double a rag five or six times; dip it in cold water and bind it on: Tried.

281. Or, bind on toasted cheese. This will cure a deep cut.

A settled Deafness

295. Take a red onion, pick out the core; fill up the place with oil of roasted almonds. Let it stand a night; then bruise and strain it. Drop three or four drops into the ear, morning and evening, and stop it with black wool.

The Ear-Ache

325. Rub the ear hard a quarter of an hour: Tried.

326. Or, be electrified.

328. Or, put in a roasted fig, or onion, as hot as may be: Tried.

329. Or, blow the smoke of tobacco strongly into it.

Dull Sight

350. Drop in two or three drops of juice of rotten apples often.

The Head-Ache

478. Rub the head for a quarter of an hour: Tried.

479. Or, be electrified: Tried.

480. Or, apply to each temple the thin yellow rind of a lemon, newly pared off.

484. Or, snuff up the nose camphorated spirits of lavender;

486. Or, a little juice of horse-radish.

A Chronical Head-Ache

488. Keep your feet in warm water a quarter of an hour before you go to bed, for two or three weeks: Tried.

489. Or, wear tender hemlock leaves under the feet, changing them daily.

490. Or, order a tea-kettle of cold water to be poured on your head, every morning, in a slender stream.

The Heart-Burning

502. Drink a pint of cold water: Tried.

509. Or, a teaspoonful of crab's eyes, ground to an impalpable powder.

The Hiccup

510. Swallow a mouthful of water, stopping the mouth and ears: Tried.

511. Or, take any thing that makes you sneeze.

514. Or three drops of oil of cinnamon on a lump of sugar: Tried.

The Itch

540. Wash the parts affected with strong rum: Tried.

544. Or, anoint them with black soap.

*545. Or, steep a shirt half an hour in a quart of water, mixed with half an ounce of powdered brimstone. Dry it slowly and wear it five or six days. Sometimes it needs repeating: Tried.

For one seemingly killed with Lightning,
a damp, or suffocated

581. Plunge him immediately into cold water.

582. Or, blow strongly with bellows down his throat. This may recover a person seemingly drowned. It is still better if a strong man blows into his mouth.

The Piles (to cure)

652. Apply warm treacle.

653. Or, a tobacco-leaf steeped in water twenty-four hours.

655. Or, a bruised onion skinned or roasted in ashes. It perfectly cures the dry piles.

The Plague (to prevent)
666. Eat marigold flowers daily, as a salad, with oil and vinegar.

The Pleurisy
675. Apply to the side, onions roasted in embers, mixed with cream.

676. Or, take half a dram of soot.

677. Or, take out the core of an apple; fill it with white frankincense; stop it close with the piece you cut out, and roast it in ashes. Mash and eat it. *I.*

A windy Rupture
729. Warm cow-dung well. Spread it thick on leather, strewing some cummin-seeds on it, and apply it hot. When cold, put on a new one. It commonly cures a child (keeping his bed) in two days.

A Sore Throat
780. Take a pint of cold water lying down in bed: Tried.

781. Or, apply a chin-stay of roasted figs.

783. Or, snuff a little honey up the nose.

784. An old sore throat was cured by living wholly upon apples and apple-water.

To clean the Teeth
867. Rub them with ashes of burnt bread.

To prevent the Tooth-Ache
868. Wash the mouth with cold water every morning and rinse them [sic] after every meal.

869. Or, rub the teeth often with tobacco ashes.

To cure the Tooth-Ache
870. Be electrified through the teeth: Tried.

871. Or, apply to the aching tooth an artificial magnet.

*878. Or, lay bruised or boiled nettles to the cheek: Tried.

880. Or, hold a slice of apple, slightly boiled, between the teeth: Tried.

Testicles inflamed
892. Boil bean-flour, in three parts water, one part vinegar. Apply it as a Poultice.

The Vertigo, or Swimming in the Head

902. Take a vomit or two.

905. Or, in a May morning about sunrise snuff up daily the dew that is on the mallow leaves.

*906. Or, apply to the top of the head, shaven, a plaister of flour of brimstone, and whites of eggs: Tried.

Warts

968. Rub them daily with a radish.

969. Or, with juice of dandelion.

970. Or, with juice of marigold-flowers: it will hardly fail.

971. Or, water in which sal armoniac is dissolved.

973. Or, apply bruised purslain as a poultice, changing it twice a day. It cures in seven or eight days.

Weakness in the Ankles

974. Hold them in cold water a quarter of an hour morning and evening.

Wounds

(If you have not an honest Surgeon at Hand)

1003. Apply juice or powder of yarrow: *I.*

1004. Or, bind leaves of ground-ivy upon it.

1007. Or keep the part in cold water for an hour, keeping the wound closed with your thumb. Then bind on the thin skin of an egg shell for days or weeks, till it falls off of itself. Regard not, though it prick or shoot for a time.

∗ I advise all in or near London, to buy their medicines at Apothecaries Hall. There they are sure to have them good.

CHAPTER 10

PRACTICAL THEOLOGIAN

When Wesley told his Conference that the purpose of God in raising up the Methodist preachers was "to reform the nation (particularly the Church) and to spread scriptural holiness across the land," he was, more than anything else, describing his own vocation. Promoting holiness was the practical goal for his every endeavor, the implicit purpose of his every activity. At the same time, he was both interested and knowledgeable in theology. The list of books he read, beginning with his early days in Oxford, contains a full range of theological works, from the writings of the early church leaders to the latest works of his contemporaries. He was, however, neither a speculative nor a systematic theologian. Theology was for him the handmaid of piety. The challenge was to put his learning into the employ of his vocation, so that the truths of the gospel might be understood and appropriated by the poor as well as the rich, the tin miner as well as the university student.

The Proclaimer of Plain Truth

Preaching was central to Wesley's vocation; his sermons are an exemplary body of Wesleyan divinity. The image of this

Oxford don, dressed in his clerical garb, standing on a miner's cart, preaching to a group of workers at Kingswood, is a fitting reminder that Wesley saw learning not as a ticket to preferment or privilege, but as a tool of his ministry to the poor. His primary congregation was the working class; his most frequent pulpit, the nearest stump or market cross. Observers of Wesley's preaching noticed that he could preach in a learned style in the churches and among great people, but "when he came among simple people, he laid all his greatness aside." The poet William Cowper is said to have described Wesley as "learned without pride." Wesley himself cultivated a "plain style" in his discourse and his writing. His design was not simple display but rather an unfolding of the grace of God.

Wesley's published sermons were for the most part written especially for publication. Of the one hundred thirty-one sermons he published during his lifetime, only fifteen bear any indication of having been preached in that specific form. Eyewitness accounts of his preaching do testify that, in some cases at least, a preached sermon might have the same basic content as a published sermon on the same text. The oral sermons, however, seem to have been longer and more anecdotal. Robert Walpole recalled that Wesley "told stories" in his sermons. Peter Williams described Wesley's preaching as "a string of mystical raptures, richly interlarded with texts of scripture and childish anecdotes about his own life and conversation." Although the published sermons are in some sense a mosaic of scriptural quotations and allusions, the anecdotal quality is not so prevalent; they probably, therefore, do not represent very well his oral style of delivery.

They do, however, contain the "essential truths of the gospel" as Wesley understood them. The practical purposes and the theological rationale for Wesley's sermons can best be seen in the preface he wrote for the first volume of his collected edition of *Sermons on Several Occasions* (1746).

PREFACE

1. The following Sermons contain the substance of what I have been preaching for between eight and nine years last past. During

This painting by William Hamilton, R.A. (1751–1801), represents Wesley in his 85th year. An entry in his *Journal* for December 22, 1787, purportedly refers to this work: "I yielded to the importunity of a painter and sat an hour and a half in all for my picture. I think it was the best that ever was taken."

that time I have frequently spoken in public, on every subject in the ensuing collection; and I am not conscious, that there is any one point of doctrine, on which I am accustomed to speak in public, which is not here, incidentally, if not professedly, laid before every Christian reader. Every serious man who peruses these, will therefore see, in the clearest manner, what these doctrines are which I embrace and teach as the essentials of true religion.

2. But I am thoroughly sensible, these are not proposed in such a manner as some may expect. Nothing here appears in an elaborate, elegant, or oratorical dress. If it had been my desire or design to write thus, my leisure would not permit. But, in truth, I, at present, designed nothing less; for I now write, as I generally speak, *ad populum,*—to the bulk of mankind, to those who neither relish nor understand the art of speaking; but who, notwithstanding, are competent judges of those truths which are necessary to present and future happiness. I mention this, that curious readers may spare themselves the labour of seeking for what they will not find.

3. I design plain truth for plain people: Therefore, of set purpose, I abstain from all nice and philosophical speculations; from all perplexed and intricate reasonings; and, as far as possible, from even the show of learning, unless in sometimes citing the original Scripture. I labour to avoid all words which are not easy to be understood, all which are not used in common life; and, in particular, those kinds of technical terms that so frequently occur in Bodies of Divinity; those modes of speaking which men of reading are intimately acquainted with, but which to common people are an unknown tongue. Yet I am not assured, that I do not sometimes slide into them unawares: It is so extremely natural to imagine, that a word which is familiar to ourselves is so to all the world.

4. Nay, my design is, in some sense, to forget all that ever I have read in my life. I mean to speak, in the general, as if I had never read one author, ancient or modern (always excepting the inspired). I am persuaded, that, on the one hand, this may be a means of enabling me more clearly to express the sentiments of my heart, while I simply follow the chain of my own thoughts, without entangling myself with those of other men; and that, on the other,

I shall come with fewer weights upon my mind, with less of prejudice and prepossession, either to search for myself or to deliver to others, the naked truths of the gospel.

5. To candid, reasonable men, I am not afraid to lay open what have been the inmost thoughts of my heart. I have thought, I am a creature of a day, passing through life as an arrow through the air. I am a spirit come from God, and returning to God: Just hovering over the great gulf; till, a few moments hence, I am no more seen; I drop into an unchangeable eternity! I want to know one thing,—the way to heaven; how to land safe on that happy shore. God himself has condescended to teach the way: For this very end he came from heaven. He hath written it down in a book. O give me that book! At any price, give me the book of God! I have it: Here is knowledge enough for me. Let me be *homo unius libri* [a person of one book]. Here then I am, far from the busy ways of men. I sit down alone: Only God is here. In his presence I open, I read his book; for this end, to find the way to heaven. Is there a doubt concerning the meaning of what I read? Does anything appear dark or intricate? I lift up my heart to the Father of Lights:—"Lord, is it not thy word, 'If any man lack wisdom, let him ask of God?' Thou 'givest liberally, and upbraidest not.' Thou hast said, 'If any be willing to do thy will, he shall know.' I am willing to do, let me know, thy will." I then search after and consider parallel passages of Scripture, "comparing spiritual things with spiritual." I meditate thereon with all the attention and earnestness of which my mind is capable. If any doubt still remains, I consult those who are experienced in the things of God; and then the writings whereby, being dead, they yet speak. And what I thus learn, that I teach.

6. I have accordingly set down in the following sermons what I find in the Bible concerning the way to heaven; with a view to distinguish this way of God from all those which are the inventions of men. I have endeavoured to describe the true, the scriptural, experimental religion, so as to omit nothing which is a real part thereof, and to add nothing thereto which is not. And herein it is more especially my desire, First, to guard those who are just setting their faces toward heaven (and who, having little acquaintance with the things of God, are the more liable to be turned out of the way) from formality, from mere outside

religion, which has almost driven heart-religion out of the world; and, Secondly, to warn those who know the religion of the heart, the faith which worketh by love, lest at any time they make void the law through faith, and so fall back into the snare of the devil.

7. By the advice and at the request of some of my friends, I have prefixed to the other sermons contained in this volume, three sermons of my own, and one of my Brother's, preached before the University of Oxford. My design required some discourses on those heads; and I preferred these before any others, as being a stronger answer than any which can be drawn up now, to those who have frequently asserted that we have changed our doctrine of late, and do not preach now what we did some years ago. Any man of understanding may now judge for himself, when he has compared the latter with the former sermons.

8. But some may say, I have mistaken the way myself, although I take upon me to teach it to others. It is probable many will think this, and it is very possible that I have. But I trust, whereinsoever I have mistaken, my mind is open to conviction. I sincerely desire to be better informed. I say to God and man, "What I know not, teach thou me!"

9. Are you persuaded you see more clearly than me? It is not unlikely that you may. Then treat me as you would desire to be treated yourself upon a change of circumstances. Point me out a better way than I have yet known. Show me it is so, by plain proof of Scripture. And if I linger in the path I have been accustomed to tread, and am therefore unwilling to leave it, labour with me a little; take me by the hand, and lead me as I am able to bear. But be not displeased if I entreat you not to beat me down in order to quicken my pace: I can go but feebly and slowly at best; then, I should not be able to go at all. May I not request of you, further, not to give me hard names in order to bring me into the right way. Suppose I were ever so much in the wrong, I doubt this would not set me right. Rather, it would make me run so much the farther from you, and so get more and more out of the way.

10. Nay, perhaps, if you are angry, so shall I be too; and then there will be small hopes of finding the truth. If once anger arise, ἠΰτε καπνός [like smoke] (as Homer somewhere expresses it,) this smoke will so dim the eyes of my soul, that I shall be able to see nothing clearly. For God's sake, if it be possible to avoid it, let us

not provoke one another to wrath. Let us not kindle in each other this fire of hell; much less blow it up into a flame. If we could discern truth by that dreadful light, would it not be loss, rather than gain? For, how far is love, even with many wrong opinions, to be preferred before truth itself without love! We may die without the knowledge of many truths, and yet be carried into Abraham's bosom. But, if we die without love, what will knowledge avail? Just as much as it avails the devil and his angels!

The God of love forbid we should ever make the trial! May he prepare us for the knowledge of all truth, by filling our hearts with all his love, and with all joy and peace in believing!

The Aspiring Perfect Christian

The plan of salvation was the focus of Wesley's preaching—the renewal of the individual in the image of God. "Christian perfection" was the keystone of his theology, the highest expression of the love of God in the soul of man. The goal of the Christian life was to "have the mind of Christ and walk as he walked." To be more explicit, the call to responsible Christian living centered for Wesley upon the Great Commandment, to love God and neighbor.

This theme of holy living, or sanctification, runs as a main thread throughout Wesley's sermons, determining both the shape of his theology and the tone of his preaching. In 1743 he wrote and published a tract which characterized "the perfect Christian," as he later said, basing his portrait on the "true Gnostic" described by Clement of Alexandria in *Stromata,* but drawing the character "in a more scriptural manner." His purpose in publishing "The Character of a Methodist" was not only to put flesh on the bones of his doctrine of Christian perfection, but also thereby to remove some prejudice from the minds of candid persons. Wesley was not hesitant to point out that the principles and practices described in this treatise were "the marks of a true Methodist—i.e. a true Christian." The equation was not accidental; within the decade he published another tract entitled "An Account of Genuine

Christianity" which was simply a portion of his defense of Methodism against the attacks of Dr. Conyers Middleton.

"The Character of a Methodist" became a fixture in the list of Methodist publications, both alluring and disarming in the simplicity and directness of its answer to the question, What are the marks of a Methodist? This work is not a description of Wesley, but rather an outline of the ideal toward which he was personally striving. As his friend Alexander Knox remarked, "to realize in himself the perfect Christian of Clemens Alexandrinus was the object of his heart." That he had not yet (or would never claim to have) reached that goal is attested in the verse prefixed to the work: "Not that I had already attained" (Phil. 3:12).

1. The distinguishing marks of a Methodist are not his opinions of any sort. His assenting to this or that scheme of religion, his embracing any particular set of notions, his espousing the judgment of one man or of another, are all quite wide of the point. Whosoever, therefore, imagines that a Methodist is a man of such or such an opinion, is grossly ignorant of the whole affair; he mistakes the truth totally. We believe, indeed, that "all Scripture is given by the inspiration of God"; and herein we are distinguished from Jews, Turks, and Infidels. We believe the written word of God to be the only and sufficient rule both of Christian faith and practice; and herein we are fundamentally distinguished from those of the Romish Church. We believe Christ to be the eternal, supreme God; and herein we are distinguished from the Socinians and Arians. But as to all opinions which do not strike at the root of Christianity, we think and let think. So that whatsoever they are, whether right or wrong, they are no distinguishing marks of a Methodist.

2. Neither are words or phrases of any sort. We do not place our religion, or any part of it, in being attached to any peculiar mode of speaking, any quaint or uncommon set of expressions. The most obvious, easy, common words, wherein our meaning can be conveyed, we prefer before others, both on ordinary occasions, and when we speak of the things of God. We never, therefore, willingly or designedly, deviate from the most usual way of speaking; unless when we express scripture truths in scripture

words, which, we presume, no Christian will condemn. Neither do we affect to use any particular expressions of scripture more frequently than others, unless they are such as are more frequently used by the inspired writers themselves. So that it is as gross an error, to place the marks of a Methodist in his words, as in opinions of any sort.

3. Nor do we desire to be distinguished by actions, customs, or usages, of an indifferent nature. Our religion does not lie in doing what God has not enjoined, or abstaining from what he hath not forbidden. It does not lie in the form of our apparel, in the posture of our body, or the covering of our heads; nor yet in abstaining from marriage, or from meats and drinks, which are all good if received with thanksgiving. Therefore, neither will any man, who knows whereof he affirms, fix the mark of a Methodist here—in any actions or customs purely indifferent, undetermined by the word of God.

4. Nor, lastly, is he distinguished by laying the whole stress of religion on any single part of it. If you say, "Yes, he is; for he thinks 'we are saved by faith alone,'" I answer, You do not understand the terms. By salvation he means holiness of heart and life. And this he affirms to spring from true faith alone. Can even a nominal Christian deny it? Is this placing a part of religion for the whole? "Do we then make void the law through faith? God forbid! Yea, we establish the law." We do not place the whole of religion (as too many do, God knoweth) either in doing no harm, or in doing good, or in using the ordinances of God. No, not in all of them together; wherein we know by experience a man may labour many years, and at the end have no religion at all, no more than he had at the beginning. Much less in any one of these; or, it may be, in a scrap of one of them: Like her who fancies herself a virtuous woman, only because she is not a prostitute; or him who dreams he is an honest man, merely because he does not rob or steal. May the Lord God of my fathers preserve me from such a poor, starved religion as this! Were this the mark of a Methodist, I would sooner choose to be a sincere Jew, Turk, or Pagan.

5. "What then is the mark? Who is a Methodist, according to your own account?" I answer: A Methodist is one who has "the love of God shed abroad in his heart by the Holy Ghost given unto him"; one who "loves the Lord his God with all his heart, and with

all his soul, and with all his mind, and with all his strength." God is the joy of his heart, and the desire of his soul; which is constantly crying out, "Whom have I in heaven but thee? and there is none upon earth that I desire beside thee! My God and my all! Thou art the strength of my heart, and my portion for ever!" . . .

9. And while he thus always exercises his love to God, by praying without ceasing, rejoicing evermore, and in everything giving thanks, this commandment is written in his heart, "That he who loveth God, love his brother also." And he accordingly loves his neighbour as himself; he loves every man as his own soul. His heart is full of love to all mankind, to every child of "the Father of the spirits of all flesh." That a man is not personally known to him, is no bar to his love; no, nor that he is known to be such as he approves not, that he repays hatred for his good-will. For he "loves his enemies"; yea, and the enemies of God, "the evil and the unthankful." And if it be not in his power to "do good to them that hate him," yet he ceases not to pray for them, though they continue to spurn his love, and still "despitefully use him and persecute him."

10. For he is "pure in heart." The love of God has purified his heart from all revengeful passions, from envy, malice, and wrath, from every unkind temper or malign affection. It hath cleansed him from pride and haughtiness of spirit, whereof alone cometh contention. And he hath now "put on bowels of mercies, kindness, humbleness of mind, meekness, longsuffering." So that he "forbears and forgives, if he had a quarrel against any; even as God in Christ hath forgiven him." And indeed all possible ground for contention, on his part, is utterly cut off. . . .

11. Agreeable to this his one desire, is the one design of his life, namely, "not to do his own will, but the will of Him that sent him." His one intention at all times and in all things is, not to please himself, but Him whom his soul loveth. He has a single eye. And because "his eye is single, his whole body is full of light." Indeed, where the loving eye of the soul is continually fixed upon God, there can be no darkness at all, "but the whole is light; as when the bright shining of a candle doth enlighten the house." . . .

12. And the tree is known by its fruits. For as he loves God, so he keeps his commandments; not only some, or most of them, but all, from the least to the greatest. He is not content to "keep the

whole law, and offend in one point"; but has, in all points, "a conscience void of offence towards God and towards man." Whatever God has forbidden, he avoids; whatever God hath enjoined, he doeth; and that whether it be little or great, hard or easy, joyous or grievous to the flesh. He "runs the way of God's commandments," now he hath set his heart at liberty. . . .

13. All the commandments of God he accordingly keeps, and that with all his might. For his obedience is in proportion to his love, the source from whence it flows. And therefore, loving God with all his heart, he serves him with all his strength. He continually presents his soul and body a living sacrifice, holy, acceptable to God; entirely and without reserve devoting himself, all he has, and all he is, to his glory. All the talents he has received, he constantly employs according to his Master's will; every power and faculty of his soul, every member of his body. . . .

14. By consequence, whatsoever he doeth, it is all to the glory of God. In all his employments of every kind, he not only aims at this (which is implied in having a single eye), but actually attains it. His business and refreshments, as well as his prayers, all serve this great end. Whether he sit in his house or walk by the way, whether he lie down or rise up, he is promoting, in all he speaks or does, the one business of his life; whether he put on his apparel, or labour, or eat and drink, or divert himself from too wasting labour, it all tends to advance the glory of God, by peace and good-will among men. His one invariable rule is this, "Whatsoever ye do, in word or deed, do it all in the name of the Lord Jesus, giving thanks to God and the Father by him."

The Prison Evangelist

Wesley's concern for the poor and the imprisoned began during the early days of Methodism at Oxford and continued throughout his life. Although he gave a great deal of time and money toward the relief of the prisoners' physical and financial problems, his primary focus was the salvation of persons, not a reform of the welfare and prison systems. William Hogarth's portrayal of a Methodist preacher reading

Wesley's *Sermons* to "The Idle Prentice" being carted off to be hanged at Tyburn is an accurate picture of the Wesleyan concern.

Wesley could not personally reach every individual in need across the country and began to use the printed word to extend his message into the nooks and crannies of society. He began to publish tracts that were designed to speak to the problems of specific groups of persons, entitling them "A Word to. . . ." The targets of the tract were a variety of sorts, including "a Drunkard," "a Swearer," "a Sabbath-Breaker," and "a Street-Walker." Among the more powerful of these pieces is "A Word to a Condemned Malefactor," spelling out the gospel message to those awaiting the hangman's noose. Although this tract is not a sermon in the usual sense, Alexander Knox's comment about Wesley's published sermons is no doubt applicable here as well: "they bear the impress and breathe the spirit of John Wesley."

[1.] What a condition are you in! The sentence is passed; you are condemned to die; and this sentence is to be executed shortly! You have no way to escape; these fetters, these walls, these gates and bars, these keepers, cut off all hope. Therefore, die you must. But must you die like a beast, without thinking what it is to die? You need not; you will not; you will think a little first; you will consider, "What is death?" It is leaving this world, these houses, lands, and all things under the sun; leaving all these things, never to return; your place will know you no more. It is leaving these pleasures; for there is no eating, drinking, gaming, no merriment in the grave. It is leaving your acquaintance, companions, friends; your father, mother, wife, children. You cannot stay with them, nor can they go with you; you must part; perhaps for ever. It is leaving a part of yourself; leaving this body which has accompanied you so long. Your soul must now drop its old companion, to rot and moulder into dust. It must enter upon a new, strange, unbodied state. It must stand naked before God!

2. But, O, how will you stand before God; the great, the holy, the just, the terrible God? Is it not his own word, "Without holiness no man shall see the Lord?" No man shall see him with joy; rather, he will call for the mountains to fall upon him, and the

rocks to cover him. And what do you think holiness is? It is purity both of heart and life. It is the mind that was in Christ, enabling us to walk as he also walked. It is the loving God with all our heart; the loving our neighbour, every man, as ourselves; and the doing to all men, in every point, as we would they should do unto us. The least part of holiness is to do good to all men, and to do no evil either in word or work. This is only the outside of it. But this is more than you have. You are far from it; far as darkness from light. You have not the mind that was in Christ: There was no pride, no malice in him; no hatred, no revenge, no furious anger, no foolish or worldly desire. You have not walked as Christ walked; no rather as the devil would have walked, had he been in a body; the works of the devil you have done, not the works of God. You have not loved God with all your heart. You have not loved him at all. You have not thought about him. You hardly knew or cared whether there was any God in the world. You have not done to others as you would they should do to you; far, very far from it. Have you done all the good you could do to all men? If so, you had never come to this place. You have done evil exceedingly; your sins against God and man are more than the hairs of your head. Insomuch that even the world cannot bear you; the world itself spews you out. Even the men that know not God declare you are not fit to live upon the earth.

3. O repent, repent! Know yourself; see and feel what a sinner you are. Think of the innumerable sins you have committed, even from your youth up. How many wicked words have you spoken? How many wicked actions have you done? Think of your inward sins; your pride, malice, hatred, anger, revenge, lust! Think of your sinful nature, totally alienated from the life of God. How is your whole soul prone to evil, void of good, corrupt, full of all abominations! Feel that your carnal mind is enmity against God. Well may the wrath of God abide upon you. He is of purer eyes than to behold iniquity: He hath said, "The soul that sinneth, it shall die." It shall die eternally, shall be "punished with everlasting destruction, from the presence of the Lord and from the glory of his power."

4. How then can you escape the damnation of hell,—the lake of fire burning with brimstone; "where the worm dieth not, and the fire is not quenched?" You can never redeem your own soul. You

cannot atone for the sins that are past. If you could leave off sin now, and live unblamable for the time to come, that would be no atonement for what is past. Nay, if you could live like an angel for a thousand years, that would not atone for one sin. But neither can you do this; you cannot leave off sin; it has the dominion over you. If all your past sins were now to be forgiven, you would immediately sin again; that is, unless your heart were cleansed; unless it were created anew. And who can do this? Who can bring a clean thing out of an unclean? Surely none but God. So you are utterly sinful, guilty, helpless! What can you do to be saved?

5. One thing is needful: "Believe in the Lord Jesus Christ, and thou shalt be saved!" Believe (not as the devils only, but) with that faith which is the gift of God, which is wrought in a poor, guilty, helpless sinner by the power of the Holy Ghost. See all thy sins on Jesus laid. God laid on him the iniquities of us all. He suffered once the just for the unjust. He bore our sins in his own body on the tree. He was wounded for thy sins; he was bruised for thy iniquities. "Behold the Lamb of God taking away the sin of the world!" taking away thy sins, even thine, and reconciling thee unto God the Father! "Look unto him and be thou saved!" If thou look unto Him by faith, if thou cleave to Him with thy whole heart, if thou receive Him both to atone, to teach, and to govern thee in all things, thou shalt be saved, thou art saved, both from the guilt, the punishment, and all the power of sin. Thou shalt have peace with God, and a peace in thy own soul, that passeth all understanding. Thy soul shall magnify the Lord, and thy spirit rejoice in God thy Saviour. The love of God shall be shed abroad in thy heart, enabling thee to trample sin under thy feet. And thou wilt then have an hope full of immortality. Thou wilt no longer be afraid to die, but rather long for the hour, having a desire to depart, and to be with Christ.

6. This is the faith that worketh by love, the way that leadeth to the kingdom. Do you earnestly desire to walk therein? Then put away all hindrances. Beware of company: At the peril of your soul, keep from those who neither know nor seek God. Your old acquaintance are no acquaintance for you, unless they too acquaint themselves with God. Let them laugh at you, or say you are running mad. It is enough, if you have praise of God. Beware of strong drink. Touch it not, lest you should not know when to

stop. You have no need of this to cheer your spirits; but of the peace and the love of God. Beware of men that pretend to show you the way to heaven, and know it not themselves. There is no other name whereby you can be saved, but the name of our Lord Jesus Christ. And there is no other way whereby you can find the virtue of his name but by faith. Beware of Satan transformed into an angel of light, and telling you it is presumption to believe in Christ, as your Lord and your God, your wisdom and righteousness, sanctification and redemption. Believe in him with your whole heart. Cast your whole soul upon his love. Trust him alone; love him alone; fear him alone; and cleave to him alone; till he shall say to you (as to the dying malefactor of old), "This day shalt thou be with me in paradise."

CHAPTER 11

PRACTICING POET

Poetic imagination seems to have been bred into the Wesley consciousness. Charles, of course, came to be known as the Poet of Methodism because of his prolific production of popular hymns. Both his father and brother Samuel wrote and published poetry, and sister Hetty's poems appeared in the *Gentleman's Magazine.* John was no exception to this family inclination toward poetic expression. From an early age, his interests and talents turned often toward poetry. When John was but twenty-one, his father wrote to him at Oxford, "I like your verses on the 65th Psalm and would not have you bury your talent." His mother, however, was a bit more circumspect: ".I would not have you leave making verses; rather make poetry sometimes your diversion, though never your business."

In keeping with these sentiments, Wesley never thought of himself primarily as a poet; but poetry was quite often for him a creative outlet. He came to see it as a useful tool for teaching and promoting Christian truth and virtue. The fascination was lifelong, the writing and reading of "pious and elegant poetry" being one of the few diversions he continued to consider appropriate to "the more excellent way." His involvement with the poetic arts took several forms: he was a reader, a collector, a writer, a translator, an editor, and a publisher of poetry.

His affinity for poetry was part of his larger fascination with language—the meaning of words, the rhythm and beauty of phrases, the direct and clear expression of ideas. Throughout his works, his carefully developed writing style weaves together classical, scriptural, and colloquial strands. This particular linguistic interest is also evident in his production of such specialized works as dictionaries of both the English and German languages and grammar textbooks for five languages.

Collector of Poetry

Poetic lines of all sorts, from epitaphs to German hymns, caught Wesley's eye. He often filled blank pages in his diaries with lines plucked from hither and yon, occasionally bawdy in the early years, usually more religious in later years. One of his early commonplace books he dedicated entirely to a collection of poetry, ranging from masterpieces of Milton and Pope to some trite, even crude, anonymous ditties. One page in his first Oxford diary became a repository for a list of fascinating colloquial expressions, probably gathered during his travels in the north country in the late 1720s. Wesley's penchant for collecting poetry was soon subsumed by his broader religious designs and reached a somewhat sanctified fruition in his publication of three volumes of *Moral and Sacred Poems* in 1744, carefully selected from many sources. Ironically, he seems to have cared more for the content of the poems than the copyright laws that protected some of them, and his literary piracy cost him £50 in legal settlements.

[From Oxford Diary I]

> Belinda has such wondrous charms,
>   Tis heaven to lie within her arms;
> And she's so charitably given
>   She wishes all mankind in heaven.

....

Tis hard, tis very hard, I swear,
   To rhyme upon a theme so bare:
Within no brains; without no hair!

. . . .

A blooming youth lies buried here,
   Euphemius to his country dear;
Nature adorned his mind and face,
   With every muse and every grace,
About the marriage state to prove
   But death had quicker wings than love!

. . . .

Part of the Provost of Aberdeen College's translation of the Bible:

Absalom was hanging in a tree
   Crying, the Lord have Marcy;
Joab came by and full angry was he,
   And run his spear up his arsy.

. . . .

[List of colloquialisms from the area around Epworth in Lincolnshire; for the meanings of many of these terms, see John Wright, English Dialect Dictionary *(1906)]*

You muckspout, you clarhkettle, I'll tan your bone-cart; ously fummart, silly kedgel; a twichel, a smooting, a blossom; rough robins, forking robins, through your ribs; as good do it soon as sins; I'm neither daunch nor divorous; in a stickle, stranny, sliving, flecked and spunged, halloking, heppen; I'll uppod ye, to gredge, smoored, bare whittle and whang; the hoggle-croggles, a hurrendurren, a dagbite, tis no raggle, rigwelted, swizzoned, to kink, bug, abboon, nawther, rattenly, to clam, to clawny, to hover, to set a gate, to remble, to threpe perseverance; murl, emse, orned, my stomach upbraids me, tull, gif, teethy, cummered, as rough as a heckle, behint, owry, obstakle, snacking, nazzarly, a bunch-clod, a nidgcock, to glog, to gausfer, to splaned [splawd?], to raum, to stocken, to spray, to quail, a gatch, thepes, grissons, hoven, kedge, to whetter, marrow, never to braid of one, to paragaud, a wike, a gime, to addle, sulky, a doubler, craply, nothing but, to fugle, to fadge, to notch, a trail-tongs, a farrand.

[From his commonplace book "Collection of Poetry" (1730)]

Upon John Dryden

At all religions, present and the past
    Thou still hast railed, yet chose the worst at last.
True to thyself; tis what thou didst before:
    Rail at all women, and then wed a whore.

. . . .

The Spider
By Mr. Pope

Artist, who underneath my table
    Thy curious texture has displaid,
Who, if we may believe the Fable
    Wast once a lovely, blooming maid:

Insidious, watchfull, restless spider,
    Fear no officious damsel's broom,
Extend thy artfull cobweb wider,
    And spread thy banner round my room.

While I thy wondrous fabric stare at
    And think on poets' haply fate,
Like thee, condemned to lonely garret
    And rudely banished rooms of state.

And as from out thy tortured body
    Thou drawst thy slender threads with pain,
So does he labour, like a noddy,
    To spin materials from his brain.

He for some tawdry, fluttering creature
    That makes a glittering in his eye;
And that's a conquest little better
    Than thine o'er captive butterfly.

Thus far, tis plain, we both agree:
    And (time perhaps may quickly show it)

Tis ten to one, but poverty
End both the spider and the poet.

....

A Collection of Moral and Sacred Poems
from the most celebrated English Authors

To the Right Honourable the Countess of Huntingdon.

Madam,

It has been a common remark, for many years, that poetry, which might answer the noblest purposes, has been prostituted to the vilest, even to confound the distinctions between virtue and vice, good and evil; and that to such a degree, that among the numerous poems now extant in our language there is an exceeding small proportion which does not, more or less, fall under this heavy censure. So that a great difficulty lies on those who are not willing, on the one hand, to be deprived of an elegant amusement, nor, on the other, to purchase it at the hazard of innocence or virtue.

Hence it is, that many have placed a chaste collection of English poems among the chief *desiderata* of this age. Your mentioning this a year or two ago, and expressing a desire to see such a collection, determined me not to delay the design I have long had of attempting something in this kind. I therefore revised all the English poems I knew and selected what appeared most valuable in them. Only Spenser's works I was constrained to omit, because scarce intelligible to the generality of modern readers.

I shall rejoice if the want of which you complained be in some measure supplied by the following collection, of which this, at least, may be affirmed: there is nothing therein contrary to virtue, nothing that can any way offend the chastest ear, or give pain to the tenderest heart. And perhaps whatever is really essential to the most sublime divinity, as well as the purest and most refined morality, will be found therein. Nor is it a small circumstance, that the most just and important sentiments are here represented with the utmost advantage, with all the ornaments both of wit and language, and in the clearest, fullest, strongest light.

Writer of Poetry

John Wesley's first published original works were poems, included in David Lewis' *Miscellaneous Poems by Several Hands* (1726). Wesley soon began to exercise this talent to produce hymns for the use of the Methodists; some of his own work appeared in the first *Collection of Psalms and Hymns* (1737) published in Charleston. Although brother Charles soon became the major source of original writing for the many collections of hymns, the brothers decided not to distinguish authorship. These publications were nearly always a joint venture, with John exercising his editorial prerogatives in almost every case, even over his brother's work. His reflections on poetry in general are expressed most concisely in the preface to the definitive collection of hymns in 1780, which he referred to as "a little body of experimental and practical divinity."

The seven former verses of the 46th Psalm
[This work was published in Lewis' Miscellaneous Poems, *and all but three stanzas were included in the Charleston collection of* Psalms and Hymns, *as they are produced here.]*

> On God supreme our hope depends,
>   Whose omnipresent sight
> Even to the pathless realms extends
>   Of uncreated night.
>
> Plunged in th' abyss of deep distress,
>   To him we raise our cry;
> His mercy bids our sorrows cease,
>   And fills our tongue with joy.
>
> Though earth her ancient seat forsake,
>   By pangs convulsive torn;
> Though her self-balanced fabric shake,
>   And ruined nature mourn:

Though hills be in the ocean lost,
  With all their shaggy load:
No fear shall e'er molest the just,
  Or shake his trust in God.

Nations remote, and realms unknown,
  In vain reject his sway;
For lo! Jehovah's voice is shown,
  And earth shall melt away.

Lest war's devouring surges rise,
  And rage on every side;
The Lord of Hosts our refuge is,
  And Jacob's God our guide.

[Written about the same time as the above, and sent to brother Samuel:]

By a cool fountain's flow'ry side
  The fair Celinda lay;
Her looks increased the summer's pride,
  Her eyes the blaze of day.

Quick through the air to this retreat
  A bee industrious flew,
Prepared to rifle every sweet
  Under the balmy dew.

Drawn by the fragrance of her breath
  Her rosy lips he found;
There in full transport sucked in death,
  And dropped upon the ground.

Enjoy, blest bee, enjoy thy fate,
  Nor at thy fall repine;
Each God would quit his blissful state
  To share a death like thine.

[The following hymn by John Wesley first appeared in the Collection of Psalms and Hymns *of 1741]*

"A Morning Hymn"

We lift our hearts to Thee,
O Day-Star from on high!
The sun itself is but Thy shade,
Yet cheers both earth and sky.

O let Thy orient beams
The night of sin disperse!
The mists of error and of vice
Which shade the universe!

How beauteous nature now!
How dark and sad before!
With joy we view the pleasing change,
And nature's God adore.

O may no gloomy crime
Pollute the rising day:
Or Jesu's blood, like evening dew,
Wash all the stains away.

May we this life improve,
To mourn for errors past,
And live this short revolving day
As if it were our last.

To God the Father, Son,
And Spirit, One and Three,
Be glory, as it was, is now,
And shall forever be.

. . . .

A Collection of Hymns
for the Use of the People Called Methodists
(1780)

PREFACE

. . . May I be permitted to add a few words with regard to the poetry? Then I will speak to those who are judges thereof with all freedom and unreserve. To these I may say, without offence: (1) In these hymns there is no doggerel, no botches, nothing put in to patch up the rhyme, no feeble expletives. (2) Here is nothing turgid or bombast on the one hand, or low and creeping on the other. (3) Here are no cant expressions, no words without meaning. Those who impute this to us know not what they say. We talk common sense, whether they understand it or not, both in verse and prose, and use no word but in a fixed and determinate sense. (4) Here are, allow me to say, both the purity, the strength, and the elegance of the English language, and, at the same time, the utmost simplicity and plainness, suited to every capacity. Lastly, I desire men of taste to judge (these are the only competent judges) whether there be not in some of the following hymns the true spirit of poetry, such as cannot be acquired by art and labour, but must be the gift of nature. By labour a man may become a tolerable imitator of Spenser, Shakespeare, or Milton, and may heap together pretty compound epithets, as *pale-eyed, meek-eyed,* and the like; but unless he be born a poet, he will never attain the genuine spirit of poetry. . . .

Translator of Poetry

John's poetical abilities also helped him translate many hymns from foreign languages, especially German. He was introduced to the Moravian hymns en route to Georgia, and his appreciation for this German poetry led him to "English" nearly three dozen of the choicest items from the Moravian hymnal, *Das Gesangbuch de Gemeinde in Herrnhuth* (1735). The hymns he chose were those he "judged to be most scriptural and most suitable to sound experience." The translation is rather free at points, so that, in spite of his stated intent to be faithful to the original text, Wesley's inclination to "improve" these lines often led to such liberties as the inclusion (in first hymn below, stanza 1, line 6) of a phrase from St. Augustine for which there is no basis either in the Tersteegen or any scriptural text.

The following selections are from among those that still

remain in the current *Book of Hymns* of The United Methodist Church. The number of stanzas, however, has often been greatly reduced from the original (bracketed stanza is from among those dropped).

"Thou Hidden Love of God" by Gerhardt Tersteegen
(1697–1769)
tr. by John Wesley

[First published in A Collection of Psalms and Hymns *(1738) with eight stanzas, of which the following are stanzas 1, 4, 6, and 8.]*

Thou hidden love of God, whose height,
  Whose depth unfathomed, no man knows,
I see from far Thy beauteous light,
  Inly I sigh for Thy repose;
My heart is pained, nor can it be
At rest, till it finds rest in Thee.

Is there a thing beneath the sun,
  That strives with Thee my heart to share?
Ah, tear it thence, and reign alone,
  The Lord of every motion there:
Then shall my heart from earth be free,
When it has found repose in Thee.

O Love, Thy sovereign aid impart,
  To save me from low-thoughted care;
Chase this self-will through all my heart,
  Through all its latent mazes there;
Make me Thy duteous child, that I
Ceaseless may, "Abba, Father," cry.

Each moment draw from earth away
  My heart, that lowly waits Thy call;
Speak to my inmost soul, and say,
  "I am thy Love, thy God, thy All!"
To feel Thy power, to hear Thy voice,
To taste Thy love, is all my choice!

"Living by Christ" by Paul Gerhardt (1607–1676)
tr. by John Wesley

[First published in Hymns and Sacred Poems *(1739) with sixteen stanzas.]*

Jesu, Thy boundless love to me
　No thought can reach, no tongue declare;
O knit my thankful heart to Thee,
　And reign without a rival there!
Thine wholly, Thine alone, I am,
Be Thou alone my constant flame.

[O grant that nothing in my soul
　May dwell, but Thy pure love alone;
O may Thy love possess me whole,
　My joy, my treasure, and my crown.
Strange fires far from my soul remove;
My every act, word, thought, be love.]

O Love, how cheering is Thy ray;
　All pain before Thy presence flies!
Care, anguish, sorrow, melt away
　Where'er Thy healing beams arise:
O Jesu, nothing may I see,
Nothing hear, feel, or think but Thee!

In suffering be Thy love my peace;
　In weakness be Thy love my power;
And when the storms of life shall cease,
　Jesu, in that important hour,
In death as life be Thou my guide,
And save me, who for me hast died!

Editor of Poetry

　Although Wesley never made poetry "his business" as such, he did get into the business of publishing poetry, as we have seen. In addition to the collections already mentioned, Wesley produced editions of some of his favorite English poets, edited in such a fashion as to be more understandable and useful to the common, unlettered people of his day. His edition of Milton's *Paradise Lost,* for instance, omitted many lines which he "despaired of explaining to the unlearned." In truth, he may also have disagreed with some of the theology in the excised portions. His tutorial instincts (presumptuousness?) combined with his pragmatic religiosity led him to alter the text in such a way as to "correct" its form. He was aiming for more simplicity and clarity while trying to do away with "mere ornamentation," intending thereby to improve the poem's practical effect—to admonish and instruct the reader.

Wesley was not the only one to try to "improve" Milton; perhaps no one succeeded. That he tried says something about his view of the arts and his role in the culture of his day. The following selections from his prefaces to extracts of Milton and Young indicate his purpose and rationale in such endeavors. The sample from *Paradise Lost* illustrates his method and technique of abridging.

An Extract from Milton's Paradise Lost

TO THE READER

Of all the poems which have hitherto appeared in the world, in whatever age or nation, the preference has generally been given, by impartial judges, to Milton's "Paradise Lost." But this inimitable work, amidst all its beauties, is unintelligible to abundance of readers: The immense learning which he has everywhere crowded together, making it quite obscure to persons of a common education.

This difficulty, almost insuperable as it appears, I have endeavoured to remove in the following extract: first, by omitting those lines which I despaired of explaining to the unlearned; and secondly, by adding short and easy notes, such as, I trust, will make the main of this excellent poem clear and intelligible to any uneducated person of a tolerable good understanding.

To those passages which I apprehend to be peculiarly excellent, either with regard to sentiment or expression, I have prefixed a star; and these, I believe, it would be worthwhile to read over and over, or even to commit to memory.

. . . .

[Milton:]

> . . . our better part remains
> To work in close design, by fraud or guile
> What force effected not: that he no less
> At length from us may find, who overcomes
> By force, hath overcome but half his foe.

[Wesley's extract:]

> . . . our better part remains
> To work by guile what force effected not:
> That he at length may find, who overcomes
> By force, hath overcome but half his foe.

. . . .

An Extract from Dr. Young's Night Thoughts on Life, Death, and Immortality

TO THE READER

. . . My design in the following extract is, (1) To leave out all the lines which seem to me, either to contain childish conceits, to sink into prosaic flatness, to rise into the turgid, the false sublime, or to be incurably obscure to common readers; (2) To explain the words which are obscure, not in themselves, but only to unlearned readers; (3) To point out, especially to these, by a single or double mark, what appear to me to be the sublimest strokes of poetry, and the most pathetic strokes of nature and passion.

It may be objected by some that I have left out too much; by others that I have left out too little. I answer, (1) I have left out no more than I apprehended to be either childish, or flat, or turgid, or obscure: So obscure as not to be explained without more words than suited with my design; (2) I have left in no more of what I conceived liable to any of these objections than was necessary to preserve some tolerable connection between the preceding and following lines.

Perhaps a more plausible objection will be that the explanations are too short. But be pleased to observe, it was no part of my design to explain anything at large; but barely to put, as often as I could, a plain word for a hard one: And where one did not occur, to use two or three, or as few as possible.

But I am sensible it may be objected farther, the word added to explain the other does not always express the meaning of it; at least, not so exactly and fully as might be. I answer, (1) I allow this; but it was the best I could find without spending more time upon it than I could afford; (2) Where the word added does not express the common meaning of the word, it often expresses the Doctor's peculiar meaning, who frequently takes words in a very uncommon, not to say improper, sense; (3) I have made a little attempt; such as I could consistently with abundance of other employment. Let one that has more leisure and more abilities supply what is here wanting.

CHAPTER 12

THE WOULD-BE HUSBAND

Wesley's long-standing ideal of celibacy (for himself) withstood several challenges during the first two decades of his ministry. Sophy Hopkey (see above, pages 97 ff.) was not the first woman to steal his heart, nor was she the last. A decade later, in his mid-forties, Wesley became convinced that "a believer might marry, without suffering loss in his soul." He was to discover, however, that tying a successful matrimonial knot was more easily rationalized than carried out. He soon became engaged to a young woman who, after a drawn-out and confusing series of events, finally married one of his preachers. Within fifteen months, John's affections had been captured by another woman, whom he rather quickly married (over the objections of his brother), only to find himself estranged from her before the decade was out. Wesley's perception of his changing "circumstances" can be seen in several documents from his own pen during this period.

The Jilted Fiance

Shortly before his brother Charles married Sarah Gwynne in April 1749, John Wesley fell in love with Grace Murray. She was a young widow thirteen years his junior whom he had employed in the Orphan House, Newcastle, to take care of the "sick and worn-out preachers." Grace had nursed Wesley back to health in August 1748, and for the next year or so directed her attentions alternately to Wesley and one of his preachers, John Bennett (who had also benefitted from her healing touch). On more than one occasion during that period, Wesley had entered into an espousal *de praesenti* with Grace, a recognized form of civil marriage contract under the current common law of England. Before Wesley could work out all the necessary conditions preliminary to the final nuptials in a church, his brother Charles had successfully and secretly intervened, seeing that Grace was married to John Bennett.

Wesley's own narrative of these events, in some ways nearly as confusing as the events themselves, gives a step-by-step description of the shifting tides of romance in this affair. It also includes an illuminating document that outlines "the grounds on which [he] had proceeded," surveying his attitudes toward the married state from the time he was a child. The holograph of this narrative is presently in the British Library, London ("An Account of an Amour of John Wesley," Add. MSS. 7119). It was published in its entirety in 1910 by J. Augustin Léger in *Wesley's Last Love*.

1. In June 1748, we had a Conference in London. Several of our brethren then objected to the *Thoughts upon Marriage,* and in a full and friendly debate convinced me that a believer might marry, without suffering loss in his soul.

2. In August following, I was taken ill at Newcastle. Grace Murray attended me continually. I observed her more narrowly than ever before, both as to her temper, sense and behaviour. I esteemed and loved her more and more. And, when I was a little recovered, I told her, sliding into it I know not how, "If ever I marry, I think you will be the person." After some time I spoke to her more directly. She seemed utterly amazed, and said, "This is too great a blessing for me: I can't tell how to believe it. This is all I could have wished for under Heaven, if I had dared to wish for it."

3. From that time I conversed with her as my own. The night before I left Newcastle, I told her, "I am convinced God has called

you to be my fellow-labourer in the Gospel. I will take you with me to Ireland in spring. Now we must part for a time. But, if we meet again, I trust we shall part no more." She begged we might not part so soon, saying, "It was more than she could bear." Upon which I took her with me through Yorkshire and Derbyshire, where she was unspeakably useful both to me and to the societies. I left her in Cheshire with John Bennett, and went on my way rejoicing.

4. Not long after I received a letter from John Bennett and another from her. He desired my consent to marry her. She said, "She believed it was the will of God." Hence I date her fall: here was the first false step, which God permitted indeed, but not approved. I was utterly amazed, but wrote a mild answer to both, supposing they were married already. She replied in so affectionate a manner, that I thought the whole design was at an end. . . .

8. We passed several months together in Ireland. I saw the work of God prosper in her hands. She lightened my burthen more than can be expressed. She examined all the women in the smaller societies and the believers in every place. She settled all the women-bands; visited the sick; prayed with the mourners, more and more of whom received remission of sins during her conversation or prayer. Meantime she was to me both a servant and friend, as well as a fellow-labourer in the Gospel. She provided everything I wanted. She told me with all faithfulness and freedom, if she thought anything amiss in my behaviour. And (what I never saw in any other to this day) she knew to reconcile the utmost plainness of speech, with such deep esteem and respect, as I often trembled at, not thinking it was due to any creature: And to join with the most exquisite modesty, a tenderness not to be expressed.

9. The more we conversed together, the more I loved her; and, before I returned from Ireland, we contracted by a contract *de praesenti:* All this while she neither wrote to J. B. nor he to her: So that the affair between *them* was as if it had never been.

10. We returned together to Bristol. It was there, or at Kingswood, that she heard some idle tales concerning me and Molly Francis. They were so plausibly related that she believed them: And in a sudden vehement fit of jealousy writ a loving letter to J. B. Of this she told me the next day in great agony of mind: but

it was too late. His passion revived: And he wrote her word, "He would meet her when she came into the North." . . .

15. The next morning, she told me what had past. I was more perplext than ever. As I now knew she loved me, and as she was contracted to me before, I knew not whether I ought to let her go? For several days I was utterly unresolved: Till on Wednesday, September 6, I put it home to herself, "Which will you choose?" and she declared again and again, "I am determined by conscience, as well as inclination, to live and die with *you.*"

16. We came to Newcastle the same evening. The next day I wrote to John Bennett. . . .

Newcastle upon Tyne, September 7, 1749.
My Dear Brother

1. The friendship between you and me has continued long. I pray God it may continue to our live's end.

But if I love you, I must deal plainly with you. And surely you desire I should. Oh that you would consider what I say! with meekness and love, and with earnest continual prayer to God!

2. You expressed a willingness some years ago, to be one of my helpers in the work of the Gospel. I gladly received you into the number, and you objected to none of the rules whereby they act. If you had, you might have continued at your own place; in friendship, though not in union, with me.

3. As one of my helpers, I desired you, three years ago, to assist me at Newcastle. In my house there I had placed a servant whom I had tried several years, and found faithful in all things. Therefore I trusted her in the highest degree, and put her in the highest office, that any woman can bear amongst us.

4. Both by the nature and rules of your office you was engaged to do nothing of importance without consulting me. She was likewise engaged by the very nature of hers, as well as by the confidence I reposed in her, to consult me in all things: to take no step of any moment, without my knowledge and consent: over and above which she was peculiarly engaged hereto, by her own voluntary and express promise.

5. Notwithstanding this, you were scarce out of my house, when without ever consulting me, you solicited her to take a step of the last importance without my consent or knowledge. You, whom I had trusted in all things, thus betrayed your trust, and moved her to do so too. You, to whom I had done no wrong, wronged me, and that in an uncommon manner. You endeavoured at the time when I expected nothing less, to rob me of a most faithful and most useful servant; the fellow to whom, for the work committed to her care, I knew not where to find in the three kingdoms.

6. Last autumn I observed her more narrowly, and perceived she was such a person, as I had sought in vain for many years, and then determined never to part with. I told her this: but told her withal, "I could not as yet proceed any farther, because I could do nothing without consulting my brother, as he had done nothing without consulting me." She answered, "It was so great a blessing that she knew not how to believe it. It seemed all as a dream." I repeated it again, and there was no shadow of objection made.

7. I told her farther, "I am convinced it is not the will of God, that you should be shut up in a corner. I am convinced you ought to labour with me in the Gospel. I therefore design to take you to Ireland in spring. Now we must separate for a season; but if we meet again, I trust we shall part no more."

And from this time, I looked upon her as my own, and resolved that nothing but death should part us.

8. Three days after I left her, without ever consulting me, you solicited her again. And in a few days more, prevailed upon her to comply, and promise marriage to *you.*

9. That very night God warned you in a vision or dream, of one who had a prior right. But whom at your instance, she pushed away. Yet you construed it in quite another manner.

10. However, thus far you went: You asked her (instead of me), "whether there was any such engagement?" Partly out of fear, partly out of love blinding her eyes, she replied, "There was not." And 'tis true, There was no explicit an engagement as would stand good in law: But such an one there was, as ought in conscience to have prevented any other, till it should be dissolved.

11. Upon her return from Ireland, God again interposed by means of those who were near you; but you construed this likewise your own way: You rushed forward, and by vehement importunity forced her tender and compassionate mind, to promise you again.

12. Now, my brother, pray earnestly that God would show you and me, what is right in this matter. Was not your very first step wrong? Was it acting faithfully, even as a friend, to move such a thing without my consent or knowledge?

Was it not much more wrong, considering you as an helper? Who as such, ought to do nothing without my advice?

Was you not hereby tempting her likewise to do extremely wrong; who was likewise engaged even as a friend, but much more as an housekeeper, to take no step, without first consulting me?

Was not all this quite unjust and unkind? as well as treacherous and unfaithful? . . .

[14.] O that you would take Scripture and reason for your rule, instead of blind and impetuous passion! I can say no more,—only this—You may tear her away by violence. But my consent I cannot, dare to give: Nor I fear can God give you his blessing.

This William Shent promised to deliver with his own hand. But it was not delivered at all.

17. In the afternoon, without any importunity or constraint, she wrote a letter to J. B. The purport of it was, "That she was more and more convinced, both he and she had sinned against God, in entering on any engagement at all, without Mr. W.'s knowledge and consent."

18. Friday, September 8, we set out for Berwick, visiting all the intermediate societies. Every hour gave me fresh proof of her usefulness on the one hand, and her affection on the other. Yet I could not consent to her repeated request, to marry immediately. I told her "before this could be done, it would be needful, 1. To satisfy J. B., 2. To procure my brother's consent, and, 3. To send an account of the reasons on which I proceed, to every helper, and every society in England, at the same time desiring their prayers." She said she should not be willing to stay above a year. I replied, "Perhaps less time will suffice." . . .

[21.] The more I knew her, the more I loved her. She frequently told me, "In time past I could have married another, if you would have given me away. But now it is impossible we should part: God has united us for ever." Abundance of conversation to the same effect, we had in our return to Newcastle: Where on Sunday 17, we continued conversing together till late at night, and she gave me all the assurances which words could give, of the most intense and inviolable affection. The same she renewed every day, yea, every hour when we were alone, unless when we were employed in prayer: which indeed took up a considerable part of the time we spent together. . . .

27. As soon as I had finished my letter to J. B. on the 7th instant, I had sent a copy of it to my brother at Bristol. The thought of my *marrying* at all, but especially of my marrying a *servant*, and one so *low-born*, appeared above measure shocking to him. Thence he inferred, that it would appear so to all mankind: and consequently, that it would break up all our societies, and put a stop to the whole work of God.

28. Full of this, instead of writing to me (who would have met him any where at the first summons) he hurried up from Bristol to Leeds. There he met with Robert Swindells, and William Shent; who informed him (which he had heard slightly mentioned before) "That G. M. was engaged to J. B." This was adding oil to the flame: So he posted to Newcastle, taking with him William Shent, not many degrees cooler than himself.

29. Here he met with Jane Keith, a woman of strong sense and exquisite subtlety. She had long been prejudiced against G. M., which had broke out more than once. She gave him just such an account as he wished to hear, and at his request, set it down in writing. The sum of it was, "1. That Mr. W. was in love with G. M. beyond all sense and reason: 2. That he had shown this in the most public manner, and had avowed it to all the society, and, 3. That all the town was in an uproar, and all the societies ready to fly in pieces."

30. My brother, believing all this, flew on for Whitehaven, concluding G. M. and I were there together. He reached it (with W. Shent) on Monday. I was not at all surprized when I saw him. He urged, "All our preachers would leave us, all our societies disperse, if I married so mean a woman." He then objected, that she was engaged to J. B. As I knew she was pre-engaged to me, as I regarded not her birth, but her qualification, and as I believed

those consequences might be prevented, I could see no valid objection yet. However I did not insist on my own judgment; but desired the whole might be preferred to Mr. Perronet which he readily consented to.

31. As soon as I was alone, I began to consider with myself, whether I was *in my senses,* or no? Whether love had *put out my eyes* (as my brother affirmed) or I had the use of them still? I weighed the steps I had taken, yet again, and the grounds on which I had proceeded. A short account of these I wrote down simply, in the following terms.

1. From the time I was six or seven years old, if any one spoke to me concerning marrying, I used to say, I thought I never should, "Because I should never find such a woman as my father had."

2. When I was about seventeen (and so till I was six or seven and twenty) I had no thought of marrying, "Because I could not keep a wife."

3. I was then persuaded, "It was unlawful for a priest to marry," grounding that persuasion on the (supposed) sense of the primitive church.

4. Not long after, by reading some of the mystic writers, I was brought to think "marriage was the less perfect state," and that there was some degree (at least) of "taint upon the mind, necessarily attending the marriage-bed."

5. At the same time I viewed in a strong light St. Paul's words to the Corinthians: And judged it "Impossible for a married man to be so without carefulness, or to attend upon the Lord with so little distraction, as a single man might do."

6. Likewise, being desirous to lay out all I could, in feeding the hungry, and clothing the naked, I could not think of marrying, "because it would bring such expence, as would swallow up all I now gave away."

7. But my grand objection for these twelve years past has been, "A dispensation of the Gospel has been committed to me. And I will do nothing which directly or indirectly tends to hinder my preaching the Gospel."

8. My first objection was easily removed by my finding some, though very few women, whom I could not but allow to be equal to my mother, both in knowledge and piety.

9. My second, "that I could not keep a wife," held only till I found reason to believe, there were persons in the world, who if I were so inclined, were both able and willing to keep *me*.

10. My third vanished away when I read with my own eyes Bp. Beveridge's *Codex Conciliorum*. I then found the very Council of Nice had determined just the contrary to what I had supposed.

11. St. Paul slowly and gradually awakened me out of my mystic dream; and convinced me, "The bed is undefiled, and no necessary hindrance to the highest perfection." Though still I did not quite shake off the weight, till our last conference in London.

12. I was next, though very unwillingly convinced, that there might be such a case as Dr. Koker's: who often declared, he was never so free from care, never served God with so little distraction, as since his marriage with one, who was both able and willing, to bear that care for him.

13. The two other objections weighed with me still, increase of expence and hindering the Gospel. But with regard to the former, I now clearly perceive, that my marriage would bring little expence, if I married one I maintain now, who would afterward desire nothing more than she had before: And would cheerfully consent, that our children (if any) should be wholly brought up at Kingswood.

14. As to the latter, I have the strongest assurance, which the nature of the thing will allow, that the person proposed would not hinder, but exceedingly further me in the work of the Gospel. For, from a close observation of several years (three of which she spent under my own roof) I am persuaded she is in every capacity an help meet for me.

15. First, as a housekeeper. . . .

16. As a nurse. . . .

17. As a companion. . . .

18. As a friend. . . .

19. Lastly, as a fellow labourer in the Gospel of Christ (the light wherein my wife is to be chiefly considered). . . .

26. But it is objected to this, [First.] That my marrying her

would turn the greater part of our preachers out of the way: insomuch that they would despise my authority, and act no more in conjunction with me.

Secondly. That it would break up our societies, and cause them to cry out, "Every man to his tents, O Israel!"

Thirdly. That it would give such scandal to the world, as never could be removed.

27. I cannot receive any one of these propositions without proof. . . .

The short is this, 1. "I have scriptural reason to marry. 2. I know no person so proper as this." . . .

42. Tuesday [Oct.] 3rd, we rode to Old-Hutton, and about 9 the next night reached Leeds. Here I found, not my brother, but Mr. Whitefield. I lay down by him on the bed. He told me, "My brother would not come, till J. B. and G. M. were married." I was troubled. He perceived it. He wept and prayed over me. But I could not shed a tear. He said all that was in his power to comfort me: But it was in vain. He told me, "It was his judgment that she was MY wife, and that he had said so to J. B.: That he would fain have persuaded them to wait, and not to marry till they had seen me: But that my brother's impetuosity prevailed and bore down all before it." . . .

44. Thurs. [Oct.] 5, about 8. One came in from Newcastle, and told us, "They were married on Tuesday." My brother came an hour after. I felt no anger. Yet I did not desire to see him. But Mr. Wh. constrained me. After a few words had past, he accosted me with, ". . . I renounce all intercourse with you, but what I would have with an heathen man or a publican." I felt little emotion. It was only adding a drop of water to a drowning man. Yet I calmly accepted his renunciation, and acquiesced therein. Poor Mr. Wh. and J. Nelson burst into tears. They prayed, cried, and intreated, till the storm past away. We could not speak, but only fell on each other's neck.

45. J. B. then came in. Neither of us could speak. But we kissed each other and wept. Soon after, I talked with my brother alone. He seemed utterly amazed. He clearly saw, I was not what he had thought, and now blamed her only: which confirmed me in believing, my presage was true, and I should see her face no more.

46. But the great mystery to me was this. By what means under heaven, could she (who I knew, whatever others thought, had for ten years loved me as her own soul) be prevailed upon to marry another? Especially after so solemn a contract with me. I could not unravel it till I read my brother's papers: what I learned from them (and some others) was this. . . .

55. On Tues. morning, Oct. 3, they were married. They all then rode on contentedly to Leeds, to give me the meeting there, as well that I might have the pleasure of seeing the bride, as "that I might acknowledge my sin" (those were my brother's expressions) before J. B. and them all.

56. But this I was not altogether ready to do. Neither did I apprehend she desired my company any more: Till on Friday Oct. 6, I was informed, "Both J. B. and his wife desired to see me." I went, But O! what an interview! It was not soon, that words could find their way. We sat weeping at each other, till I asked her, "What did you say to my brother, to make him accost me thus?" She fell at my feet: said "She never had spoke, nor could speak against me:" uttering many other words to the same effect, in the midst of numberless sighs and tears. Before she rose, he fell on his knees too, and asked my pardon for what he had spoken of me. Between them both, I knew not what to say or do. I can forgive. But who can redress the wrong?

57. After dinner I talked with her alone. She averred with the utmost emotion, being all dissolved in tears, "That she never laid the blame on me, whom she knew to be wholly innocent: That she would rather die than speak against one, to whom she had so deep obligations. That at the time I first spoke to her at Newcastle, she loved me above all persons living: that after her engagement with J. B. her heart was divided till she went to Ireland: that then it was whole with me, and from that time, till J. B. met us at Epworth: that after his speaking she was divided again, till I talked with her on the road; from which hour she loved me more and more, till we parted at Hineley-Hill: That, when my brother took her thence, she thought he was carrying her to me: that, when she knew more of his design, she told him, "I will do nothing, till I have seen Mr. W.":" But that when it was told her at Newcastle, among a thousand other things, "Mr. W. will have nothing to say to you," then she said, "Well, I will have Mr. B. if he will have me." If these

things are so, hardly has such a case been from the beginning of the world!

The New Husband

John Wesley married Mary Vazeille in February 1751. There is no known record of where the ceremony occurred or who officiated. The marriage notices in the *Gentleman's Magazine* include the following simple statement:

Feb. 18—Rev. Mr. John Wesley, methodist preacher, — to a merchant's widow in Threadneedle-street, with a jointure [inherited annuity] of £300 per annum.

Charles had been "thunderstruck" when he found out his brother was "resolved to marry," and had "groaned" for several days at the prospect of John's decision and the effect it would have on Methodism. But John had become clearly convinced and now "fully believed that, in my present circumstances, I might be more useful in a married state." Charles was also surprised at John's choice of a bride; if Grace Murray had been unsatisfactory in Charles' eyes because of her lowly state as a servant, this wealthy widow ranked little higher.

Charles had little opportuity to meddle in this case, however. Barely two weeks after John had announced his marital intentions to his brother, he was married. John's plans had been accelerated when, on Sunday, February 10, 1751, he accidentally slipped on the ice while crossing London Bridge and sprained his foot. He recuperated at Mrs. Vazeille's, spending his time, as he later reported, "partly in prayer, reading, and conversation, and partly in writing a Hebrew grammar and *Lessons for Children*." After a week or so (the *London Magazine* gives the date as February *19*), John and Mary were married.

The newly married Wesley was back on the job before his foot was healed, preaching on the 19th and 20th from a kneeling position. A fortnight later, being "tolerably able to ride, though not to walk," he set out for Bristol for a conference of the preachers, leaving his wife in London. He returned to London for six days in March before setting out for an eight-week journey to Scotland and the North Country. His *Journal* notes at this point, "I cannot understand how a Methodist preacher can answer it to God to preach one sermon or travel one day less in a married than in a single state. In this respect surely 'it remaineth that they who have wives be as though they had none.'"

The following letters, written during those first two tours away from home, not only express Wesley's genuine affection but also show his unequivocal view of his wife's duties and obligations in his absence.

Bristol, March 11, 1751

And can my dear Molly spend four whole days, Friday, Saturday, Sunday, and Monday, without saying one word to me? However, you will forgive me if I am not so patient. I want to be talking to you, if not with you. I want to converse a little in the only way which is now allowed me. My body is stronger and stronger—and so is my love to you. God grant it may never go beyond his will! O that we may always continue to love one another as Christ loved us!

Do you neglect none of your temporal business? Have you wrote to Spain? And sold your jewels? And settled with Mr. Blisson? And does my dear Jenny continue to press forward? Do not you forget the poor? Have you visited the prison? My dear, be not angry that I put you upon so much work. I want you to crowd all your life with the work of faith and the labour of love. How can we ever do enough for him that has done and suffered so much for us? Are not you willing to suffer also for him? To endure the contradiction of sinners? Surely you are willing to bear whatever his wise Providence permits to fall upon you.

Let your own heart tell you what mine feels, when I bless God that I am

Ever yours.

Manchester, April 7, 1751

Last night I had the pleasure of receiving two letters from my dearest earthly friend. I can't answer them till I tell you how I love you—though you knew it before. You feel it in your own breast. For (thanks be to God) your heart is as my heart. And in token of it you have given me your hand.

If you find yourself at any time heavy for a season, you know where to go for help. You will cry without delay:

Take this poor, flutt'ring heart to rest,
And lodge it, Saviour, in thy breast!

In June, if it please God to continue our life and health, you shall travel with me. I want to have you always near me. And yet even that want is made easy. I was glad you was not with me last week. For it has rained every day. . . .

I think you might have found a better husband. But Oh! where could I have found so good a wife? If I was not to bless God, surely the stones would cry out!

I suppose you mean Miss Mady Perronet. I am glad she is with you. I love her dearly. Nevertheless it will be inconvenient on some accounts. To prevent which inconveniences you will quit your house (if you live) at midsummer. We agree in desiring to cut off every needless expense. O how exactly your heart agrees with mine! Thanks be to God for this unspeakable gift.

My dear soul, adieu!

The Rejected Husband

Wesley's friend Alexander Knox once wrote, "It is certain that Mr. Wesley had a predilection for the female character, . . . partly from his generally finding in females a quicker and fuller responsiveness to his own ideas of interior piety and affectionate devotion." For Knox, such a preference explained why Wesley wrote "with peculiar effluence of thought and frankness of communication" to a wide range of female correspondents. One further observation by Knox is telling: "He so literally *talks* upon paper as to make it inconceivable that he should have conversed with them in any other style than that in which he wrote to them."

Molly Wesley seems to have had similar feelings about her husband John's correspondence with women. But she apparently was not quite so willing as Knox to see Wesley's literary expressions of affection as being entirely "pure and paternal." Among a growing list of marital tensions, the problems of privacy and trust were among the major issues that eventually drew the marriage asunder.

Molly took the first initiative toward separation; she left John on several occasions, beginning in 1757. John's attitude toward his wife's departure in one instance is illustrated by a comment in his journal: *"Non eam reliqui; non dimisi, non revocabo* [I did not leave her; I did not send her away, I shall not call her back]."

He did, however, send letters after her, spelling out the problems as he understood them and outlining the conditions under which harmony could be restored. If these letters are indeed an example of the way Wesley would have conversed in this situation, one can easily understand why Mrs. Wesley spent much of the last few years of her life away from her husband. Likewise, if there is any truth to his assertions, one can easily understand why he did not call her back.

Coleford, October 23, 1759

Dear Molly,—I will tell you simply and plainly the things which I dislike. If you remove them, well. If not, I am but where I was. I dislike (1) Your showing any one my letters and private papers without my leave. This never did any good yet, either to you or me or any one. It only sharpens and embitters your own spirit. And the same effect it naturally has upon others. The same it would have upon me, but that (by the grace of God) I do not think of it. It can do no good. It can never bring me nearer, though it may drive me farther off. . . .

I dislike (2) Not having the command of my own house, not being at liberty to invite even my nearest relations so much as to drink a dish of tea without disobliging *you.* I dislike (3) The being myself a prisoner in my own house; the having my chamber door watched continually so that no person can go in or out but such as have your good leave. I dislike (4) The being but a prisoner at large, even when I go abroad, inasmuch as you are highly disgusted if I do not give you an account of every place I go to and every person with whom I converse. I dislike (5) The not being safe in my own house. My house is *not* my castle. I cannot call even my study, even my bureau, my own. They are liable to be plundered every day. You say, "I plunder you of nothing but papers." I am not sure of that. How is it possible I should? I miss money too, and he that will steal a pin will steal a pound. But were it so, a scholar's papers are his treasure—my Journal in particular. "But I took only such papers as relate to Sarah Ryan and Sarah Crosby." That is not true. What are Mr. Landey's letters to them? Besides, you have taken parts of my Journal which relate to neither one nor the other. I dislike (6) Your treatment of my servants (though, indeed, they are not properly mine). You do all that in you lies to make their lives a burthen to them. You browbeat, harass, rate them like dogs, make them afraid to speak to me. You treat them with such haughtiness, sternness, sourness, surliness, ill-nature, as never were known in any house of mine for near a dozen years. You forget even good breeding, and use such coarse language as befits none but a fishwife.

I dislike (7) Your talking against me behind my back, and that every day and almost every hour of the day; making my faults (real or supposed) the standing topic of your conversation. I dislike (8) Your slandering me, laying to my charge things which you know are false. Such are (to go but a few days back)—that I beat you, which you told James Burges; that I rode to Kingswood with Sarah Ryan, which you told Sarah Crosby; and that I required you, when we were first married, never to sit in my presence without my leave, which you told Mrs. Lee, Mrs. Fry, and several others, and stood it before my face. I dislike (9) Your common custom of saying things not true. To instance only in two or three particulars. You told Mr. Ireland "Mr. Vazeille learnt Spanish in a fortnight." You told Mr. Fry "Mrs. Ellison was the author as to my intrigue in Georgia." You told Mrs. Ellison "you never said any such thing; you never charged her with it." You also told her "that I had laid a plot to serve you as Susannah was served by the two elders." I dislike (10) Your extreme, immeasurable bitterness to all who endeavour to defend my character (as my brother, Joseph Jones, Clayton Carthy), breaking out even into foul, unmannerly language, such as ought not to defile a gentlewoman's lips if she did not believe one word of the Bible.

And now, Molly, what would any one advise you to that has a real concern for your happiness? Certainly (1) to show, read, touch those letters no more, if you did not restore them to their proper owner; (2) to allow *me* the command of my own house, with free leave to invite thither whom I please; (3) to allow me my liberty there that any who will may come to me without let or hindrance; (4) to let me go where I please and to whom I please without giving an account to any; (5) to assure me you will take no more of my papers nor anything of mine without my consent; (6) to treat all the servants where you are, whether you like them or no, with courtesy and humanity, and to speak (if you speak at all) to them, as well as others, with good nature and good manners; (7) to speak no evil of me behind my back; (8) never to accuse me falsely; (9) to be extremely cautious of saying anything that is not strictly true, both as to the matter and manner; and (10) to avoid all bitterness of expression till you can avoid all bitterness of spirit.

These are the advices which I now give you in the fear of God and in tender love to your soul. Nor can I give you a stronger proof that I am

Your affectionate Husband

....

York, July 15, 1774

My Dear,—1. I think it needful to write one letter more in order to state the case between you and me from the beginning. I can't, indeed, do this so exactly as I would, because I have not either those letters or those parts of my Journal which give a particular account of all circumstances just as they occurred. I have therefore only my memory to depend on; and that is not very retentive of evil. So that it is probable I shall omit abundance of things which might have thrown still more light on the subject. However, I will do as well as I can, simply relating the fact to the best of my memory and judgment.

2. Before we married I saw you was a well-bred woman of great address and a middling understanding; at the same time I believed you to be of a mild, sweet, and even temper. By conversing with you twenty days after we were married, I was confirmed in the belief. Full of this, I wrote to you soon after our first parting in the

openness and simplicity of my heart. And in this belief I continued after my return till we went down to Kingswood.

3. Here, as I came one morning into your room, I saw a sight which I little expected. You was all thunder and lightning: I stared and listened; said little, and retired. You quickly followed me into the other room, fell upon your knees, and asked my pardon. I desired you to think of it no more, saying, It is with *me* as if it had never been. In two or three weeks, you relapsed again and again, and as often owned your fault, only with less and less concern. You first found we were *both* in fault, and then all the fault was on *my side.*

4. We returned to London, and your natural temper appeared more and more. In order to soften it as I could, I tried every method I could devise. Sometimes I reasoned with you at large, sometimes in few words. At other times I declined argument, and tried what persuasion would do. And many times I heard all you said, and answered only by silence. But argument and persuasion, many words and few, speaking and silence, were all one. They made no impression at all. One might as well attempt to convince or persuade the north wind.

5. Finding there was no prevailing upon you by speaking, I tried what writing would do. And I wrote with all plainness; yet in as mild a manner as I could, and with all the softness and tenderness I was master of. But what effect did it produce? Just none at all; you construed it all into ill-nature, and was not easily prevailed upon to *forgive* so *high an affront.*

6. I think your quarrel with my brother was near this time, which continued about seven years; during two or three of which it was more or less a constant bone of contention between us, till I told you plainly, "I dare not sit and hear my brother spoken against. Therefore, whenever you begin to talk of him, I must rise and leave the room."

7. In the midst of this you drew new matter of offence from my acquaintance with Mrs. Lefevre, a dove-like woman, full of faith and humble love and harmless as a little child. I should have rejoiced to converse with her frequently and largely; but for *your* sake I abstained. I did not often talk with her at all, and visited her but twice or thrice in two years. Notwithstanding which, though you sometimes said you thought her a good woman, yet at other

times you did not scruple to say you "questioned if I did not lie with her." And afterward you seemed to make no question of it.

8. Some time after, you took offence of my being so much with Mrs. Blackwell, and was "sure she did me no good." But this blew over, and you was often in a good humour for a week together, till October 1757. Sarah Ryan, the housekeeper at Bristol, then put a period to the quarrel between my brother and you. Meantime she asked me once and again, "Sir, should I sit and hear Mrs. Wesley talk against *you* by the hour together?" I said, "Hear her, if you can thereby do her any good." A while after, she came to me and said, "Indeed, sir, I can bear it no longer. It would wound my own soul." Immediately you was violently jealous of her, and required me not to speak or write to her. At the same time you insisted on the "liberty of opening and reading all letters directed to me." This you had often done before: but I still insisted on my own liberty of speaking and writing to whom I judged proper; and of seeing my own letters first, and letting you read only those I saw fit.

9. Sunday, February 25, 1758, you went into my study, opened my bureau, and took many of my letters and papers. But on your restoring most of them two days after, I said, "Now, my dear, let all that is past be forgotten; and if either of us find any fresh ground of complaint, let us tell it to Mr. Blackwell, or Jo. Jones, or Tho. Walsh, but to no other person whatever." You agreed; and on Monday, March 6, when I took my leave of you to set out for Ireland, I thought we had as tender a parting as we had had for several years.

10. To confirm this good understanding, I wrote to you a few days after all that was in my heart. But from your answer I learned it had a quite contrary effect: you *resented* it deeply; so that for ten or twelve weeks together, though I wrote letter after letter, I received not one line. Meantime you told Mrs. Vigor and twenty more, "Mr. Wesley *never* writes to *me*. You must inquire concerning him of Sarah Ryan; he writes to her *every week*." So far from it, that I did not write to her at all for above twelve weeks before I left Ireland. Yet I really thought you would not tell a wilful lie—at least, not in cold blood; till poor, dying T. Walsh asked me at Limerick, "How did you part with Mrs. W. the last time?" On my saying, "Very affectionately," he replied, "Why, what a woman is this! She told me your parting words were, 'I hope to see

your wicked face no more.'" I now saw you was resolved to blacken me at all events, and would stick at no means to accomplish it. Nevertheless I laboured for peace; and at my return to Bristol, to avoid grieving *you,* did not converse with Sarah Ryan (though we were in the same house) twenty minutes in ten days' time. I returned to London. Soon after, you grew jealous of Sarah Crosby, and led me a weary life, unless I told you every place to which I went and every person I saw there.

11. Perceiving you still rose in your demands, I resolved to break through at once, and to show you I would be my own master, and go where I pleased, without asking any one's leave. Accordingly on Monday, December 18, I set out for Norwich; the first journey I had taken since we were married without telling you where I was going.

I cannot but add a few words: not by way of reproach, but of advice. God has used many means to curb your stubborn will and break the impetuosity of your temper. He has given you a dutiful but sickly daughter; He has taken away one of your sons. Another has been a grievous cross; as the third probably will be. He has suffered you to be defrauded of much money; He has chastened you with strong pain. And still He may say, "How long liftest thou up thyself against Me?" Are you more humble, more gentle, more patient, more placable than you was? I fear quite the reverse; I fear your natural tempers are rather increased than diminished. O beware lest God give you up to your own heart's lusts, and let you follow your own imaginations!

Under all these conflicts it might be an unspeakable blessing that you have an husband who knows your temper and can bear with it; who, after you have tried him numberless ways, laid to his charge things that he knew not, robbed him, betrayed his confidence, revealed his secrets, given him a thousand treacherous wounds, purposely aspersed and murdered his character, and made it your *business* so to do, under the poor pretence of vindicating your own character (whereas of what importance is *your* character to mankind, if you was buried just now? or if you had never lived, what loss would it be to the cause of God?);—who, I say, after all these provocations, is still willing to forgive you all; to overlook what is past, as if it had not been, and to receive you with open arms; not only while you have a sword in your hand, with which you are continually striking at me, though you cannot hurt me. If, notwithstanding, you continue striking at me still, what can I, what can all reasonable men think, but that either you are utterly out of your senses or your eye is not single; that you married me only for my money; that, being disappointed, you was almost always out of humour; that this laid you open to a thousand suspicions, which, once awakened, could sleep no more?

My dear Molly, let the time past suffice. If you have not (to prevent my giving it to bad women) robbed me of my substance too; if you do not blacken me, on purpose that when this breaks out, no one may believe it; stop, and consider what you do. As yet the breach may be repaired; you have wronged me much, but not beyond forgiveness. I love you still, and am as clear from all other women as the day I was born. At length know *me,* and know *yourself.* Your enemy I cannot be; but let me be your friend. Suspect me no more; asperse me no more; provoke me no more. Do not any longer contend for mastery, for power, money, or praise. Be content to be a private, insignificant person, known and loved by God and me. Attempt no more to abridge me of the liberty which I claim by the laws of God and man. Leave *me* to be governed by God and my own conscience. Then shall I govern *you* with gentle sway, and show that I do indeed love you, even as Christ the Church.

These charges and the scandalous periods of separation contributed to Mrs. Wesley's growing reputation among the Methodist people as "a troubler of their happiness and peace." She begged her husband to "put a stop to this torrent of evil that is poured out against me." At best, John's attitude was only conditionally compromising. The two strong-minded individuals never resolved their differences satisfactorily. Mrs. Wesley ended her days living apart from John. She died on October 8, 1781; John was out of town. Although he returned to London on the day of her burial, Wesley was not informed of it until a day or two later.

CHAPTER 13

THE ANXIOUS EARTHEN VESSEL

The Modest Epitaph Writer

From a very early age, Wesley was conscious of that fragile thread called health, upon which life itself depended. Although he lived to a ripe old age, he was well aware that any serious illness might signal the approach of his last days. With that specter in mind, he quite frequently paused on his birthday to reflect upon his health, in his later years noting in particular when his vigor and vitality were as those of a man thirty years his junior. His consciousness of the fragility of life is reflected in many *Journal* references to sudden deaths, often followed by words like "such a vapour is life" (cf. James 4:14) or some other wistful comment. In some cases, he uses those occasions to admonish readers to be sure to make a will, if they have not done so already!

Wesley's diaries and his published *Journal* contain numerous references to physical problems (noted in the daily diaries under the summary of God's providential acts evident for that day, which also included the weather), from "spitting blood" and "lameness" during his Oxford days to "impetuous flux" and "seasickness" in his later years. One particularly serious bout with illness took place late in 1753, not only preventing him from preaching for four months, but also inspiring him to write his own epitaph. His friend George Whitefield wrote a letter to Wesley upon hearing of "the apparent approach of his dissolution": "If in the land of the dying [i.e., not yet *dead*], I hope to pay my last respects to you next week. If not, Rev. and very dear Sir, F-a-r-e-w-e-ll. . . . My heart is too big, tears trickle down too fast."

Wesley's own account of this illness is contained in his *Journal* for 1753.

Sat. [Nov.] 24—I rode home, and was pretty well till night, but my cough was then worse than ever. My fever returned at the same time, together with the pain in my left breast; so that I should probably have stayed at home on Sunday the 25th had it not been advertised in the public papers that I would preach a charity sermon at the chapel, both morning and afternoon. My cough did not interrupt me while I preached in the morning, but it was extremely troublesome while I administered the sacrament. In the afternoon I consulted my friends whether I should attempt to preach again or no. They thought I should, as it had been advertised. I did so, but very few could hear. My fever increased much while I was preaching; however, I ventured to meet the society, and for near an hour my voice and strength were restored, so that I felt neither pain nor weakness.

Mon. 26—Dr. Fothergill told me plain, I must not stay in town a day longer, adding, "If anything does thee good, it must be the country air, with rest, asses' milk, and riding daily." So (not being able to sit a horse) about noon I took coach for Lewisham.

In the evening (not knowing how it might please God to dispose of me), to prevent vile panegyric, I wrote as follows:

HERE LIETH THE BODY
OF
JOHN WESLEY
A BRAND PLUCKED OUT OF THE BURNING:
WHO DIED OF A CONSUMPTION
IN THE FIFTY-FIRST YEAR OF HIS AGE,
NOT LEAVING, AFTER HIS DEBTS ARE PAID,
TEN POUNDS BEHIND HIM:
PRAYING,
GOD BE MERCIFUL TO ME,
AN UNPROFITABLE SERVANT!

Wesley published this portrait of himself (artist unknown) in *The Arminian Magazine* (1783), an odd choice in the light of his expressed desire in 1780 for "striking likenesses in the *Magazine*" (see above, pages 14 and 25).

Wed. 28—I found no change for the better, the medicines which had helped me before now taking no effect. About noon (the time that some of our brethren in London had set apart for joining in prayer) a thought came into my mind to make an experiment. So I ordered some stone brimstone to be powdered, mixed with the white of an egg, and spread on brown paper, which I applied to my side. The pain ceased in five minutes, the fever in half an hour, and from this hour I began to recover strength. The next day I was able to ride, which I continued to do every day till January 1. Nor did the weather hinder me once, it being always tolerable fair (however it was before) between twelve and one o'clock.

An Honest Heathen

Wesley's lifelong quest for self-knowledge was not a superficial exercise. In his own spiritual pilgrimage, Wesley's attempt to "press on to perfection" seems to be marked by a continuing desire for a sense of assurance. The first experience of assurance in 1738 seems not to have had an abiding satisfaction for his heart, as we saw above (page 102). The periods of despair and *angst* became less frequent but apparently no less intense as time went on. A comment to his brother in 1772 is telling: "I often cry out, *Vitae me redde priori!* [Let me return to my former life!] Let me be again an Oxford Methodist! I am often in doubt whether it would not be best for me to resume all my Oxford rules, great and small."

The following letter was written by John to his brother Charles during a period when the Methodist movement was experiencing a great deal of upheaval and tension. Sections transcribed from shorthand are shown in brackets.

Whitehaven, June 27, 1766

Dear Brother,—I think you and I have abundantly too little intercourse with each other. Are we not *old acquaintances?* Have we not known each other for half a century? and are we not jointly engaged in such a work as probably no two other men upon earth are? Why, then, do we keep at such a distance? It is a mere device of Satan. But surely we ought not at this time of day to be ignorant of his devices. Let us therefore make the full use of the little time that remains. *We* at least should *think aloud* and use to the uttermost the light and grace on each bestowed. We should help each other,

Of little life the best to make,
And manage wisely the last stake.

In one of my last I was saying I do not feel the wrath of God abiding on me; nor can I believe it does. And yet (this is the mystery) [I do not love God. I never did]. Therefore [I never] believed in the Christian sense of the word. Therefore [I am only an] honest heathen, a proselyte of the Temple, one of the Φοβούμενοι τὸν Θεόν [God-fearers]. And yet to be so employed of God! and so hedged in that I can neither get forward nor backward! Surely there never was such an instance before, from the beginning of the world! If I [ever have had] *that faith,* it would not be so strange. But [I never had any] other ἔλεγχος [evidence] of the eternal or invisible world than [I have] now; and that is [none at all], unless such as faintly shines from reason's glimmering ray. [I have no] direct witness, I do not say that [I am a child of God], but of anything invisible or eternal.

And yet I dare not preach otherwise than I do, either concerning faith, or love, or justification, or perfection. And yet I find rather an increase than a decrease of zeal for the whole work of God and every part of it. I am Φερόμενος [borne along], I know not how, that I can't stand still. I want all the world to come to ὃν οὐκ οἶδα [what I do not know]. Neither am I impelled to this by fear of any kind. I have no more fear than love. Or if I have [any fear, it is not that of falling] into hell but of falling into nothing.

I hope you are with Billy Evans. If there is an Israelite indeed, I think he is one. O insist everywhere on *full* redemption, receivable by *faith alone!* Consequently to be looked for *now.* You are *made,* as it were, for this very thing. Just here you are in your element. In connexion I beat you; but in strong, pointed sentences you beat me. Go on, in your *own way,* what God has peculiarly called you to. Press the *instantaneous* blessing: then I shall have more time for my peculiar calling, enforcing the *gradual* work.

We must have a thorough *reform of the preachers.* I wish you would *come to Leeds* with John Jones in the machine. It comes in two days; and after staying two days, you might return. I would willingly bear your expenses up and down. I believe it will help, not hurt, your health.

My love to Sally.

CHAPTER 14

THE CATHOLIC
AND ANTI-CATHOLIC SPIRIT

Wesley often appears to be a very opinionated person; he was not hesitant to defend his religious and political views against an opposing position. As an Englishman of the eighteenth century, he shared many of the prejudices of the contemporary English temper, including the long-standing bias against Roman Catholics. However, Wesley did not adopt the total antipathy toward papists typical of the period. As the leader of a minority religious movement that experienced persecution, Wesley might be expected to favor and promote toleration wherever and whenever possible. He was therefore quite willing to extend an olive branch to Roman Catholics in Ireland, pointing to the common ground they shared as Christians. This did not lessen either his own convictions on theological matters or his own feelings about the political threat that the papists posed in England.

The Irenic Theologian

Wesley faced many mobs. The motives of these riotous gangs were quite varied, but religious prejudice was often one springboard that helped incite them to action. In Ireland, some of the crowds that attacked Wesley and the Methodists contained large numbers of "Romanists." In 1749, during his third visit to Ireland, he wrote both his *Short Address to the Inhabitants of Ireland,* an apology for Methodism in the face of previous opposition and disturbances, and his *Letter to a Roman Catholic,* an appeal for mutual respect and cooperation. In spite of the possible motive of self-preservation (that could have prompted such a letter to *any* religious group that joined his opposition), Wesley exhibits an ecumenical sensitivity in both the tone and the content of this *Letter* that exceeds what one might expect under those circumstances and has had far-reaching implications for more recent ventures in ecumenical cooperation.

To a Roman Catholic

Dublin, July 18, 1749

1. You have heard ten thousand stories of us who are commonly called Protestants, of which, if you believe only one in a thousand, you must think very hardly of us. But this is quite contrary to our Lord's rule, "Judge not, that ye be not judged"; and has many ill consequences, particularly this—it inclines us to think as hardly of you. Hence we are on both sides less willing to help one another, and more ready to hurt each other. Hence brotherly love is utterly destroyed; and each side, looking on the other as monsters, gives way to anger, hatred, malice, to every unkind affection, which have frequently broke out in such inhuman barbarities as are scarce named among the heathens.

2. Now, can nothing be done, even allowing us on both sides to retain our own opinions, for the softening our hearts towards each other, the giving a check to this flood of unkindness, and restoring at least some small degree of love among our neighbours and countrymen? Do not you wish for this? Are you not fully convinced that malice, hatred, revenge, bitterness, whether in us or in you, in our hearts or yours, are an abomination to the Lord? Be our opinions right, or be they wrong, these tempers are undeniably wrong. They are the broad road that leads to destruction, to the nethermost hell.

3. I do not suppose all the bitterness is on your side. I know

there is too much on our side also—so much, that I fear many Protestants (so called) will be angry at me too for writing to you in this manner, and will say, "It is showing you too much favour; you deserve no such treatment at our hands."

4. But I think you do. I think you deserve the tenderest regard I can show, were it only because the same God hath raised you and me from the dust of the earth, and has made us both capable of loving and enjoying Him to eternity; were it only because the Son of God has bought you and me with His own blood. How much more, if you are a person fearing God (as without question many of you are) and studying to have a conscience void of offence towards God and towards man!

5. I shall therefore endeavour, as mildly and inoffensively as I can, to remove in some measure the ground of your unkindness, by plainly declaring what our belief and what our practice is; that you may see we are not altogether such monsters as perhaps you imagined us to be.

A true Protestant may express his belief in these or the like words:—

6. As I am assured that there is an infinite and independent Being, and that it is impossible there should be more than one; so I believe that this one God is the Father of all things, especially of angels and men; that He is in a peculiar manner the Father of those whom He regenerates by His Spirit, whom He adopts in His Son as co-heirs with Him, and crowns with an eternal inheritance; but in a still higher sense the Father of His only Son, whom He hath begotten from eternity.

I believe this Father of all, not only to be able to do whatsoever pleaseth Him, but also to have an eternal right of making what and when and how He pleaseth, and of possessing and disposing of all that He has made; and that He of His own goodness created heaven and earth and all that is therein.

7. I believe that Jesus of Nazareth was the Saviour of the world, the Messiah so long foretold; that, being anointed with the Holy Ghost, He was a Prophet, revealing to us the whole will of God; that He was a Priest, who gave Himself a sacrifice for sin, and still makes intercession for transgressors; that He is a King, who has all power in heaven and in earth, and will reign till He has subdued all things to Himself.

I believe He is the proper, natural Son of God, God of God, very God of very God; and that He is the Lord of all, having absolute, supreme, universal dominion over all things; but more peculiarly our Lord, who believe in Him, both by conquest, purchase, and voluntary obligation.

I believe that He was made man, joining the human nature with the divine in one person; being conceived by the singular operation of the Holy Ghost, and born of the blessed Virgin Mary, who, as well after as before she brought Him forth, continued a pure and unspotted virgin.

I believe He suffered inexpressible pains both of body and soul, and at last death, even the death of the cross, at the time that Pontius Pilate governed Judaea under the Roman Emperor; that His body was then laid in the grave, and His soul went to the place of separate spirits; that the third day He rose again from the dead; that He ascended into heaven; where He remains in the midst of the throne of God, in the highest power and glory, as Mediator till the end of the world, as God to all eternity; that in the end He will come down from heaven to judge every man according to his works, both those who shall be then alive and all who have died before that day.

8. I believe the infinite and eternal Spirit of God, equal with the Father and the Son, to be not only perfectly holy in Himself, but the immediate cause of all holiness in us; enlightening our understandings, rectifying our wills and affections, renewing our natures, uniting our persons to Christ, assuring us of the adoption of sons, leading us in our actions, purifying and sanctifying our souls and bodies, to a full and eternal enjoyment of God.

9. I believe that Christ by His Apostles gathered unto Himself a Church, to which He has continually added such as shall be saved; that this catholic (that is, universal) Church, extending to all nations and all ages, is holy in all its members, who have fellowship with God the Father, Son, and Holy Ghost; that they have fellowship with the holy angels, who constantly minister to these heirs of salvation; and with all the living members of Christ on earth, as well as all who are departed in His faith and fear.

10. I believe God forgives all the sins of them that truly repent and unfeignedly believe His holy gospel; and that at the last day all men shall rise again, every one with his own body.

I believe that, as the unjust shall after their resurrection be tormented in hell for ever, so the just shall enjoy inconceivable happiness in the presence of God to all eternity.

11. Now, is there anything wrong with this? Is there any one point which you do not believe as well as we?

But you think we ought to believe more. We will not now enter into the dispute. Only let me ask, If a man sincerely believes thus much, and practises accordingly, can any one possibly persuade you to think that such a man shall perish everlastingly?

12. "But does he practise accordingly?" If he does not, we grant all his faith will not save him. And this leads me to show you in a few and plain words what the practise of a true Protestant is.

I say, a true Protestant: for I disclaim all common swearers, Sabbath-breakers, drunkards; all whoremongers, liars, cheats, extortioners; in a word, all that live in open sin. These are no Protestants; they are no Christians at all. Give them their own name: they are open heathens. They are the curse of the nation, the bane of society, the shame of mankind, the scum of the earth.

13. A true Protestant believes in God, has a full confidence in His mercy, fears Him with a filial fear, and loves Him with all his soul. He worships God in spirit and in truth, in everything gives Him thanks; calls upon Him with his heart as well as his lips at all times and in all places; honours His holy name and His Word, and serves Him truly all the days of his life.

Now, do not you yourself approve of this? Is there any one point you can condemn? Do not you practise as well as approve it? Can you ever be happy, if you do not? Can you ever expect true peace in this or glory in the world to come, if you do not believe in God through Christ? if you do not thus fear and love God? My dear friend, consider, I am not persuading you to leave or change your religion, but to follow after that fear and love of God without which all religion is vain. I say not a word to you about your opinions or outward manner of worship. But I say, all worship is an abomination to the Lord, unless you worship Him in spirit and in truth, with your heart as well as your lips, with your spirit and with your understanding also. Be your form of worship what it will, but in everything give Him thanks, else it is all but lost labour. Use whatever outward observances you please; but put your whole trust in Him, but honour His holy name and His Word, and serve Him truly all the days of your life.

14. Again: a true Protestant loves his neighbour—that is, every man, friend or enemy, good or bad—as himself, as he loves his own soul, as Christ loved us. And as Christ laid down His life for us, so is he ready to lay down his life for his brethren. He shows this love by doing to all men in all points as he would they should do unto him. He loves, honours, and obeys his father and mother, and helps them to the uttermost of his power. He honours and obeys the King, and all that are put in authority under him. He cheerfully submits to all his governors, teachers, spiritual pastors, and masters. He behaves lowly and reverently to all his betters. He hurts nobody by word or deed. He is true and just in all his dealings. He bears no malice or hatred in his heart. He abstains from all evil-speaking, lying, and slandering; neither is guile found in his mouth. Knowing his body to be the temple of the Holy Ghost, he keeps it in sobriety, temperance, and chastity. He does not desire other men's goods; but is content with that he hath, labours to get his own living, and to do the whole will of God in that state of life unto which it has pleased God to call him.

15. Have you anything to reprove in this? Are you not herein even as he? If not (tell the truth), are you not condemned both by God and your own conscience? Can you fall short of any one point hereof without falling short of being a Christian?

Come, my brother, and let us reason together. Are you right, if you only love your friend and hate your enemy? Do not even the heathens and publicans so? You are called to love your enemies, to bless them that curse you, and to pray for them that despitefully use you and persecute you. But are you not disobedient to the heavenly calling? Does your tender love to all men—not only the good, but also the evil and unthankful—approve you the child of your Father which is in heaven? Otherwise, whatever you believe and whatever you practise, you are of your father the devil. Are you ready to lay down your life for your brethren? and do you do unto all as you would they should do unto you? If not, do not deceive your own soul: you are but a heathen still. Do you love, honour, and obey your father and mother, and help them to the utmost of your power? Do you honour and obey all in authority? all your governors, spiritual pastors, and masters? Do you behave lowly and reverently to all your betters? Do you hurt nobody by word or deed? Are you true and just in all your dealings? Do you take care to pay whatever you owe? Do you feel no malice, or envy, or revenge, no hatred or bitterness to any man? If you do, it is plain you are not of God; for all these are the tempers of the devil. Do you speak the truth from your heart to all men, and that in tenderness and love? Are you an "Israelite indeed, in whom is no guile"? Do you keep your body in sobriety, temperance, and chastity, as knowing it is the temple of the Holy Ghost, and that, if any man defile the temple of God, him will God destroy? Have you learned, in every state wherein you are, therewith to be content? Do you labour to get your own living, abhorring idleness as you abhor hell-fire? The devil tempts other men; but an idle man tempts the devil: an idle man's brain is the devil's shop, where he is continually working mischief. Are you not slothful in business? Whatever your hand finds to do, do you do it with your might? And do you do all as unto the Lord, as a sacrifice unto God, acceptable in Christ Jesus?

This, and this alone, is the old religion. This is true, primitive Christianity. Oh, when shall it spread over all the earth? when shall it be found both in us and you? Without waiting for others, let each of us by the grace of God amend one.

16. Are we not thus far agreed? Let us thank God for this, and receive it as a fresh token of his love. But if God still loveth us, we ought also to love one another. We ought, without this endless jangling about opinions, to provoke one another to love and to good works. Let the points wherein we differ stand aside: here are enough wherein we agree, enough to be the ground of every Christian temper and of every Christian action.

O brethren, let us not still fall out by the way! I hope to see you in heaven. And if I practise the religion above described, you dare not say I shall go to hell. You cannot think so. None can persuade you to it. Your own conscience tells you the contrary. Then, if we cannot as yet think alike in all things, at least we may love alike. Herein we cannot possibly do amiss. For of one point none can doubt a moment,—"God is love; and he that dwelleth in love, dwelleth in God, and God in him."

17. In the name, then, and in the strength of God, let us resolve, first, not to hurt one another; to do nothing unkind or unfriendly to

each other, nothing which we would not have done to ourselves. Rather let us endeavour after every instance of a kind, friendly and Christian behaviour towards each other.

Let us resolve, secondly, God being our helper, to speak nothing harsh or unkind of each other. The sure way to avoid this is to say all the good we can both of and to one another; in all our conversation, either with or concerning each other, to use only the language of love, to speak with all softness and tenderness, with the most endearing expression which is consistent with truth and sincerity.

Let us, thirdly, resolve to harbour no unkind thought, no unfriendly temper, towards each other. Let us lay the axe to the root of the tree; let us examine all that rises in our heart, and suffer no disposition there which is contrary to tender affection. Then shall we easily refrain from unkind actions and words, when the very root of bitterness is cut up.

Let us, fourthly, endeavour to help each other on in whatever we are agreed leads to the kingdom. So far as we can, let us always rejoice to strengthen each other's hands in God. Above all, let us each take heed to himself (since each must give an account of himself to God) that he fall not short of the religion of love, that he be not condemned in that he himself approveth. O let you and I (whatever others do) press on to the prize of our high calling! that, being justified by faith, we may have peace with God through our Lord Jesus Christ; that we may rejoice in God through Jesus Christ, by whom we have received the atonement; that the love of God may be shed abroad in our hearts by the Holy Ghost which is given unto us. Let us count all things but loss for the excellency of the knowledge of Jesus Christ our Lord; being ready for Him to suffer the loss of all things, and counting them but dung, that we may win Christ.—I am

Your affectionate servant for Christ's sake.

Protestant Patriot

Wesley was a man of his times. Nowhere is this more obvious than in his reaction to the Relief Act of 1778 that relaxed the laws against Roman Catholics. Wesley had a typically English fear of "popery" and its potential threat to the well-being of the English state.

This deep-seated bias did not necessarily negate the "Catholic spirit" exhibited in the letter in the previous section and in the sermon of that title. Wesley was convinced that no contradiction existed between his openness to religious dialogue with the Roman Catholics and his argument against their "intolerant, persecuting principles." His support of Lord George Gordon's controversial Protestant Association, however, disappointed many, whose fears were realized when the Gordon riots erupted less than six months later.

This letter, published in *The Public Advertiser* (1780), was reprinted as a broadsheet. Wesley noted in his *Journal,* "Many were grievously offended, but I cannot help it; I must follow my own conscience."

To the Printer of the PUBLIC ADVERTISER.

Sir,

Some time ago a pamphlet was sent me entitled, "An Appeal from the Protestant Association, to the People of Great Britain." A day or two since a kind of answer to this was put into my hand, which pronounces "its style contemptible, its reasoning futile, and its object malicious." On the contrary, I think the style of it is clear, easy and natural; the reasoning (in general) strong and conclusive; the object, or design, kind and benevolent. And in pursuance of the same kind and benevolent design, namely, to preserve our happy constitution, I shall endeavour to confirm the substance of that tract, by a few plain arguments.

With persecution I have nothing to do. I persecute no man for his religious principles. Let there be as "boundless a freedom in religion," as any man can conceive. But this does not touch the point: I will set religion, true or false, utterly out of the question. Suppose the Bible, if you please, to be a fable, and the Koran to be the word of God. I consider not, whether the Romish religion to be true or false; I build nothing on one or the other suppositions. Therefore away with all your commonplace declamation about intolerance and persecution for religion! Suppose every word of Pope *Pius's* creed to be true; suppose the Council of *Trent* to have been infallible: yet, I insist upon it, that no government not Roman Catholic ought to tolerate men of the Roman Catholic persuasion.

I prove this by a plain argument; (let him answer it that can)—That no Roman Catholic does or can give security for his allegiance or peaceable behaviour, I prove thus. It is a Roman Catholic maxim established not by private men, but by a public council, that "no faith is to be kept with heretics." This has been openly avowed by the Council of *Constance:* but it never was openly disclaimed (whether private persons avow or disavow it). It is a fixed maxim of the Church of *Rome*. But as long as it is so, nothing can be more plain, than that the memebers of that Church can give no reasonable security to any government of their allegiance or peaceable behaviour. Therefore, they ought not to be tolerated by any government, Protestant, Mahometan, or pagan.

You may say, "Nay, but they will take an *Oath* of Allegiance." True, five hundred oaths; but the maxim, "No faith is to be kept with heretics," sweeps them all away as a spider's web. So that still, no governors that are not Roman Catholics can have any security of their allegiance.

Again, those who acknowledge the *spiritual power* of the pope can give no security of their allegiance to any government; but all Roman Catholics acknowledge this: therefore, they can give no security for their allegiance.

The power of granting *pardons* for all sins, past, present, and to come, is and has been for many centuries one branch of his *spiritual power.*

But those who acknowledge him to have this spiritual power, can give no security for their allegiance: since they believe the pope can pardon rebellions, high treason, and all other sins whatsoever.

The power of *dispensing* with any promise, oath or vow, is another branch of the *spiritual power* of the pope. And all who acknowledge his spiritual power, must acknowledge this. But whoever acknowledges the *dispensing power* of the pope, can give no security of his allegiance to any government.

Oaths and promises are none: they are light as air, a dispensation makes them all null and void.

Nay, not only the pope, but even a priest, has *power to pardon sins!*—This is an essential doctrine of the Church of Rome. But they that acknowledge this, cannot possibly give any security for their allegiance to any government. Oaths are no security at all; for the priest can pardon both perjury and high treason.

Setting then religion aside, it is plain, that upon principles of reason, no government ought to tolerate men, who cannot give any security to that government, for their allegiance and peaceable behaviour. But this no Romanist can do, not only while he holds that "No faith is to be kept with heretics," but so long as he acknowledges either priestly absolution, or the *spiritual power* of the pope.

"But the late act, you say, does not either *tolerate* or *encourage* Roman Catholics." I appeal to matter of fact. Do not the Romanists themselves understand it as a toleration? You know they do. And does it not already (let alone what it *may* do by and by) *encourage* them to preach openly, to build chapels (at Bath and elsewhere), to raise seminaries, and to make numerous converts day by day to their intolerant, persecuting principles? I can point out, if need be, several of the persons. And they are increasing daily.

But "nothing dangerous to English liberty is to be apprehended from them." I am not certain of that. Some time since a Romish priest came to one I knew: and after talking with her largely, broke out, "You are no heretic! You have the experience of a real Christian!" "And would you," she asked, "burn me alive?" He said, "God forbid!—Unless it were for the good of the Church!"

Now what security could she have had for her life, if it had depended on that man? The *good of the Church* would have burst all the ties of truth, justice, and mercy. Especially when seconded by the absolution of a priest, or (if need were) a papal pardon.

If any one please to answer this, and to set his name, I shall probably reply.—But the productions of anonymous writers, I do not promise to take any notice of.

I am, sir, your humble servant,
JOHN WESLEY

City Road, Jan. 21, 1780.

CHAPTER 15

THE CAREFUL PLANNER

John Wesley was the all-important link in the Methodist "connexion." He, more than anyone else, knew the possibly disastrous implications this held for the future of the movement. By the 1760s, the chances of maintaining a vital and continuing alliance with the evangelical wing of the Church of England were becoming increasingly dim. Many tensions seemed to be pulling the connexion apart into a congregational system. Wesley saw the preachers themselves as the key to any perpetuation of their "union." His outlook toward the future settled into two types of proposals: the establishment of some form of council, and/or the designation of a single successor to his position.

The Center of Union

As early as 1760, Wesley had suggested the possibility of establishing a council to guide Methodism. The council would, of course, only come into power after his death. Wesley again spelled out the idea in 1769 in a letter "To the Traveling Preachers," later reprinted in the "Large" Minutes (1770). This letter exhibits the particular concerns that Wesley had in mind as he looked to the future of Methodism as a continuing order of lay preachers within the Church of England.

Leeds, August 4, 1769

My dear brethren,

1. It has long been my desire that all those ministers of our Church who believe and preach salvation by faith might cordially agree between themselves, and not hinder but help one another. After occasionally pressing this in private conversation wherever I had opportunity, I wrote down my thoughts upon the head and sent them to each in a letter. Out of fifty or sixty to whom I wrote, only three vouchsafed me an answer. So I give this up; I can do no more. They are a rope of sand, and such they will continue.

2. But it is otherwise with the travelling preachers in our Connexion. You are at present one body. You act in concert with each other and by united counsels. And now is the time to consider what can be done in order to continue this union. Indeed, as long as I live there will be no great difficulty. I am under God a center of union to all our travelling as well as local preachers.

They all know me and my communication. They all love me for my work's sake; and therefore, were it only out of regard to me, they will continue connected with each other. But by what means may this connexion be preserved when God removes me from you?

3. I take it for granted it cannot be preserved by any means between those who have not a single eye. Those who aim at anything but the glory of God and the salvation of men, who desire or seek any earthly thing, whether honour, profit, or ease, will not, cannot continue in the Connexion; it will not answer their design. Some of them, perhaps a fourth of the whole number, will secure preferment in the Church. Others will turn Independents, and get separate congregations, like John Edwards and Charles Skelton. Lay your accounts with this, and be not surprised if some you do not suspect be of this number.

4. But what method can be taken to preserve a firm union between those who choose to remain together? Perhaps you might take some such steps as these:

On notice of my death, let all the preachers in England and Ireland repair to London within six weeks.

Let them seek God by solemn fasting and prayer.

Let them draw up articles of agreement to be signed by those who choose to act in concert.

Let those be dismissed who do not choose it in the most friendly manner possible.

Let them choose by votes a committee of three, five, or seven, each of whom is to be Moderator in his turn.

Let the Committee do what I do now; propose preachers to be tried, admitted, or excluded; fix the place of each preacher for the ensuing year and the time of the next Conference.

5. Can anything be done now in order to lay a foundation for this future union? Would it not be well, for any that are willing, to sign some articles of agreement before God calls me hence? Suppose something like these:

"We whose names are under-written, being thoroughly convinced of the necessity of a close union between those whom God is pleased to use as instruments in this glorious work, in order to preserve this union between ourselves, are resolved, God being our Helper,

I. *To devote ourselves entirely to God,* denying ourselves, taking up our cross daily, steadily aiming at one thing—to save our own souls and them that hear us.

II. *To preach the old Methodist doctrines,* and no other, contained in the *Minutes* of the Conferences.

III. To observe and enforce the whole *Methodist discipline* laid down in the said *Minutes.*"

The Perpetual Image

As time went on, Wesley increasingly felt that a strong union among the preachers depended upon their having a single strong leader. As he approached his seventieth birthday, he decided to designate a successor. John William Fletcher was his choice.

Fletcher was the vicar of Madeley and one of the few Church of England clergy still connected with Methodism in 1773. Fletcher was proving himself equal to the challenges of leadership, not least of all by writing a series of *Checks to Antinomianism* (1771–1775) that defended Wesley's theology against the Calvinist attack. He was also considered by Wesley to be without equal in piety.

This letter to Fletcher is a telling indicator of Wesley's expectations for the future leaders of Methodism. The description Wesley gives may, in fact, have been patterned after his perception of his own role in the movement, perhaps (though not necessarily) idealized. At that point, Fletcher was probably the best choice Wesley could have made; unfortunately Fletcher died before Wesley. The movement was entrusted in the end to the Conference by the Deed of Declaration (1784).

Shoreham, January [15], 1773

Dear Sir,—What an amazing work has God wrought in these kingdoms in less than forty years! And it not only continues but increases throughout England, Scotland, and Ireland; nay, it has lately spread into New York, Pennsylvania, Virginia, Maryland, and Carolina. But the wise men of the world say, "When Mr. Wesley drops, then all this is at an end!" And so it surely will unless, before God calls him hence, one is found to stand in his place. For οὐκ ἀγαθὸν πολυκοιρανίη εἰς κοίρανος ἔστω [the rule of many is not good; let there be one ruler]. I see more and more, unless there be one προεδτώς [leader], the work can never be carried on. The body of the preachers are not united; nor will any part of them submit to the rest: so that either there must be *one* to preside over *all* or the work will indeed come to an end.

But who is sufficient for these things? qualified to preside both over the preachers and people? He must be a man of faith and love and one that has a single eye to the advancement of the kingdom of God. He must have a clear understanding; a knowledge of men and things, particularly of the Methodist doctrine and discipline; a ready utterance; diligence and activity, with a tolerable share of health. There must be added to these, favour with the people, with the Methodists in general. For unless God turn their eyes and their hearts towards him, he will be quite incapable of the work. He must likewise have some degree of learning; because there are many adversaries, learned as well as unlearned, whose mouths must be stopped. But this cannot be done unless he be able to meet them on their own ground.

But has God provided one so qualified? Who is he? *Thou art the man!* God has given you a measure of loving faith and a single eye to His glory. He has given you some knowledge of men and things, particularly of the whole plan of Methodism. You are blessed with some health, activity, and diligence, together with a degree of learning. And to all these He has lately added, by a way none could have foreseen, favour both with the preachers and the whole people.

Come out in the name of God! Come to the help of the Lord against the mighty! Come while I am alive and capable of labour!

> *Dum superest Lachesi quod torqueat, et pedibus me*
> *Porto meis, nullo dextram subeunte bacillo.*

[While Lachesis has some thread of life to spin,
And I walk on my own feet, without the help of a staff.]
Come while I am able, God assisting, to build you up to faith, to ripen your gifts, and to introduce you to the people. *Nil tanti* [Nothing is worth so much]. What possible employment can you have which is of *so great importance*?

But you will naturally say, "I am not equal to the task; I have neither grace nor gifts for such an employment." You say true; it is certain you have not. And who has? But do you not know *Him* who is able to give them? perhaps not at once, but rather day by day: as each is, so shall your strength be.

"But this implies," you may say, "a thousand crosses, such as I feel I am not able to bear." You are not able to bear them now; and they are not now come. Whenever they do come, will He not send them in due number, weight, and measure? And will they not all be for your profit, that you may be a partaker of His holiness?

Without conferring, therefore, with flesh and blood, come and strengthen the hands, comfort the heart, and share the labour of
Your affectionate friend and brother.

The Philanthropic Testator

Fully aware of the transitory nature of existence, Wesley had made a will as early as 1747, following the advice he often gave to his people. Two decades later, he prepared an updated version that included his wife among his beneficiaries (see Tyerman, *Life of Wesley,* II, 15 f.). His final will, drawn up in 1789, is concerned primarily with the disposition of his books, manuscripts, and personal belongings.

Wesley had often been accused of having an income greater than that of an Anglican bishop (see volume 2, page 76 n.). But his own principle with regard to money was not only to "gain all you can" and to "save all you can," but also to "give all you can." His estate consisted primarily of his books and publishing interests, the income from which was designated for the use of the Methodist connexion. He had once said, in his *Earnest Appeal* (1745), that if he left more than ten pounds at his death, any one could call him a thief and a robber (cf. his proposed epitaph above, page 196). In his last will, given below, the only money directly dispersed was the six pounds to be given to the six poor people who were to be his pallbearers, and the money in his bureau and pockets to be divided among his wife's grandchildren and four other friends. The value of his property, however, appears to have been rather substantial.

In the name of God, Amen.

I, John Wesley, Clerk, sometime Fellow of Lincoln College, Oxford, revoking all others, appoint this to be my last Will and Testament.

I give all my books, now on sale, and the copies of them (only subject to a rent-charge of eighty-five pounds a year to the widow and children of my brother), to my faithful friends, John Horton, merchant; George Wolff, merchant; and William Marriott, stockbroker, all of London, in trust for the general Fund of the Methodist Conference in carrying on the work of God by Itinerant Preachers; on condition that they permit the following Committee, Thomas Coke, James Creighton, Peard Dickinson, Thomas Rankin, George Whitfield, and the London Assistant for the time being, still to superintend the printing-press, and to employ Hannah Paramore and George Paramore, as heretofore, unless four of the Committee judge a change to be needful.

I give the books, furniture, and whatever belongs to me in the

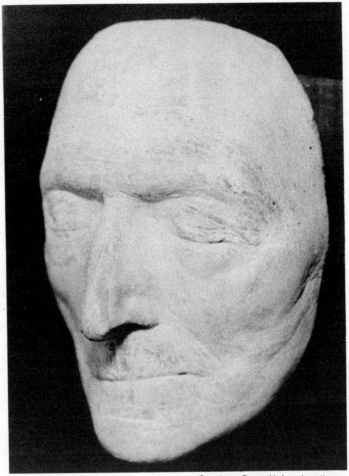

Wesley's death mask, a plaster facial cast taken shortly after his death in 1791. Although visual representations of Wesley vary greatly, the prominent nose is one of the common features in nearly every portrayal.

three houses at Kingswood, in trust to Thomas Coke, Alexander Mather, and Henry Moore, to be still employed in teaching and maintaining the children of poor Travelling Preachers.

I give to Thomas Coke, Doctor John Whitehead, and Henry Moore, all the books which are in my study and bedchamber at London, and in my studies elsewhere, in trust, for the use of the Preachers who shall labour there from time to time.

I give the coins, and whatever else is in the drawer of my bureau at London, to my dear grand-daughters, Mary and Jane Smith.

I give all my manuscripts to Thomas Coke, Doctor Whitehead, and Henry Moore, to be burned or published as they see good.

I give whatever money remains in my bureau and pockets, at my decease, to be equally divided between Thomas Briscoe, William Collins, John Easton, and Isaac Brown.

I desire my gowns, cassocks, sashes, and bands may remain at the chapels for the use of the clergymen attending there.

I desire the London Assistant for the time being to divide the rest of my wearing apparel between those four of the Travelling Preachers that want it most; only my pelisse I give to the Rev. Mr. Creighton; my watch to my friend Joseph Bradford; my gold seal to Elizabeth Ritchie.

I give my chaise and horses to James Ward and Charles Wheeler, in trust, to be sold, and the money divided, one half to Hannah Abbott, and the other to the poor members of the select society.

Out of the first money which arises from the sale of books, I bequeath to my dear sister, Martha Hall (if alive), forty pounds; to Mr. Creighton aforesaid, forty pounds; and to the Rev. Mr. Heath, sixty pounds.

And whereas I am empowered by a late Deed to name the persons who are to preach in the new chapel in London (the Clergymen for continuance), and by another Deed to name a Committee for appointing Preachers in the new chapel at Bath, I do hereby appoint John Richardson, Thomas Coke, James Creighton, Peard Dickinson, Clerks; Alexander Mather, William Thompson, Henry Moore, Andrew Blair, John Valton, Joseph Bradford, James Rogers, and William Myles, to preach in the new chapel at London, and to be the Committee for appointing Preachers in the new chapel at Bath.

I likewise appoint Henry Brooke, painter; Arthur Keene, gent.; and William Whitestone, stationer, all of Dublin, to receive the annuity of five pounds (English), left to Kingswood School by the late Roger Shiel, Esq.

I give six pounds to be divided among the six poor men, named by the Assistant, who shall carry my body to the grave; for I particularly desire there may be no hearse, no coach, no escutcheon, no pomp, except the tears of them that loved me, and are following me to Abraham's bosom. I solemnly adjure my Executors, in the name of God, punctually to observe this.

Lastly, I give to each of those Travelling Preachers who shall remain in the Connexion six months after my decease, a little token of my love, the eight volumes of sermons.

I appoint John Horton, George Wolff, and William Marriott, aforesaid, to be Executors of this my last Will and Testament; for which trouble they will receive no recompense till the resurrection of the just.

Witness my hand and seal, the 20th day of February, 1789.

JOHN WESLEY (Seal.)

Signed, sealed, and delivered, by the said Testator, as and for his last Will and Testament, in the presence of us,

WILLIAM CLULOW,
ELIZABETH CLULOW.

Should there be any part of my personal estate undisposed of by this my Will, I give the same unto my two nieces, Elizabeth Ellison and Susanna Collett, equally.

JOHN WESLEY.

WILLIAM CLULOW,
ELIZABETH CLULOW.

Feb. 25, 1789.

I give my types, printing-presses, types [sic], and everything pertaining thereto, to Mr. Thomas Rankin and Mr. George Whitfield, in trust, for the use of the Conference.

JOHN WESLEY.